CONFIDENTIAL

SUPREME HEADQUARTERS ALLIED
EXPEDITIONARY FORCE
EVALUATION AND DISSEMINATION SECTION
G-2 (COUNTER INTELLIGENCE SUB-DIVISION)

THE
NSFK OF THE NSDAP

E.D.S./G/2

CONFIDENTIAL

SUPREME HEADQUARTERS ALLIED
EXPEDITIONARY FORCE
EVALUATION AND DISSEMINATION SECTION
G-2 (COUNTER INTELLIGENCE SUB-DIVISION)

THE
NSFK OF THE NSDAP

E.D.S./G/2

Published by

The Naval & Military Press Ltd
Unit 5 Riverside, Brambleside
Bellbrook Industrial Estate
Uckfield, East Sussex
TN22 1QQ England

Tel: +44 (0)1825 749494

www.naval-military-press.com
www.nmarchive.com

In reprinting in facsimile from the original, any imperfections are inevitably reproduced and the quality may fall short of modern type and cartographic standards.

ERRATA:-

NSFK of the NSDAP

Page 11, paragraph 18: in line 23, for

"NSKK-Obergruppenführer" read "NSFK-Obergruppenführer".

Page 11, paragraph 19: in paragraph heading, for

"NSKK" read "NSFK".

Page 11, paragraph 19: in line 1, for

"NSKK-Korpsführung" read "NSFK-Korpsführung".

CONFIDENTIAL

SUPREME HEADQUARTERS ALLIED EXPEDITIONARY FORCE
EVALUATION AND DISSEMINATION SECTION
G-2 (COUNTER INTELLIGENCE SUB-DIVISION)

B-A-S-I-C   H-A-N-D-B-O-O-K

THE NSFK

(Das Nationalsozialistische Fliegerkorps)

NATIONAL SOCIALIST AVIATION

CORPS

E.D.S./G/2
   Compiled by MIRS (LONDON Branch)
   From Material Available at
   WASHINGTON and LONDON.

TABLE OF CONTENTS

NOTE: Abbreviations used in NSFK documents will largely correspond with those used in SA documents. No list has, therefore, been included in this publication; reference should be made to the Basic Handbook of the SA (E.D.S./G/1).

		Page
	Foreword	1

PART I

ORIGIN AND DEVELOPMENT

1	Status	2
2	Development	3
3	Primary Functions	3

PART II

TRAINING AND RECRUITING

4	The NSFK and the Hitler Youth	4
5	Training with Model Planes	4
6	Training in the Flieger HJ	5
7	Glider Training: Certificates and Badges	5
8	Further Training of the Flieger HJ	6
9	Wireless Training	7
10	Workshop Training	7
11	Parachute Training	7
12	NSFK Membership	7
13	Honorary Membership	8
14	Changes During the War	8
15	The NSFK and the Luftwaffe	9

PART III

ORGANISATION AND STRENGTH

16	Group Organisation	10
17	Organisation: Standarten and Below	10
18	NSFK Commanders	11
19	NSFK High Command HQ	11
20	Schools and Training Centres	12
21	Strength	14

PART IV

UNIFORMS AND RANKS

22	Uniforms	15
23	Ranks and Insignia	16

ANNEXE A

(Order of Battle Tables)

Key	A 1
PART ONE: NSFK Gruppen	A 2
PART TWO: NSFK Standarten	A 7

ANNEXE B

Organisation of the NSFK	Diagram
Uniforms of the NSFK	Plates

ANNEXE C

Gazetteer	C

ANNEXE D

Who's Who	D

ANNEXE E

Captured OB	E

FOREWORD

The National-Socialist Aviation Corps represents the only Party sponsored formation which, although not considered a Parteigliederung (Party formation), is to a far reaching degree under Party patronage, thoroughly indoctrinated and yet under the direct control of the German Air Ministry.

In other words it is chronologically the first, and one of the most direct, bridges between the Nazi Party and the Wehrmacht.

A clear borderline between Luftwaffe and NSFK personnel, at least with regard to Training Centres, can no longer be drawn today. It must be considered Germany's foremost training agency for the Luftwaffe, having trained 8,000 of the Reich's 18,000 pilots by September, 1939.

The NSFK has established in Greater Germany at least 1,000 headquarters (down to company level), and over 60 highly specialised aviation schools and training centres.

It is noteworthy that the NS Aviation Corps, (and its then yet unorganised predecessors), constituted the primary means by which the Third Reich (and prior to 1933, under the Weimar Republic, the Reichswehr, German industry and the Nationalist Right-wing factions of Germany) managed to evade and circumvent the Versailles Treaty disarmament clauses pertaining to the air force.

From an occupational counter-intelligence point of view the regional network of the NSFK may well be considered an establishment easily transformed into an organised set-up to function as a source of disaffection.

Nazi "ideological camaraderie" is especially evident in the units of this formation and it is certain the NSFK may boast a particularly strong grip on Germany's youth.

PART I

ORIGINS AND DEVELOPMENT

1. **Status**

The National Socialist Aviation Corps was founded by a decree of 17 April 1937. According to it the Deutsche Luftsport-Verband (German Air Sport League) and all its Gruppen (groups) were dissolved, the NSFK taking its place.

Furthermore, the ukase signed by Hitler stated that the NSFK was a "Körperschaft des" öffentlichen Rechtes (a "legally registered, state-controlled corporation") under the command of the Korpsführer des NSFK (Commander-in-Chief) who in turn is subordinated to the Reichsminister für Luftfahrt (Reich Air Minister).

Nazi Party publications, as well as the German public regard the NSFK as a Gliederung (formation) of the Nazi Party not unlike e.g. the SA (Storm Troops), SS (Black Elite Guards) or NSKK (National Socialist Motor Corps). The NSFK is even accorded preferential status. A special order decrees that no German may simultaneously hold membership in more than one of these formations, and specifies that "service in the NSFK enjoys preference; whosoever is fit for the NSFK and desires admission into this formation, is to be transferred to it"

Nevertheless, the NSFK is not a Parteigliederung (Nazi Party Formation) but a "public body" and almost, in fact, a branch of the German Air Ministry. Decrees defining the status of full-time professional NSFK functionaries (hauptämtlich Bedienstete) stress this in such publications as the Reichsarbeitsblatt (National Labour Gazette).

The Korpsführer is directly responsible to the Reich Air Minister and Commander-in-Chief of the Air Force (GÖRING) rather than to the Reichsleitung der NSDAP (the Directorate of the Nazi Party). However, Göring's control of the Korpsführer from a party point of view may be likened e.g. to that of a Reichsleiter (member of the Supreme Party Directorate) to a party affiliation.

The following reasons may be cited for the preferential status of the NSFK:
   (a) The National Socialist State and its leaders have always been specially air-minded and have at all times stressed the importance of aviation for Germany. The following quotation from GÖRING is the motto of the NSFK: "Das deutsche Volk muss ein Volk von Fliegern werden". (The German people must become a nation of aviators).
   (b) The NSFK was created much later than the SA, SS or NSKK, at a time when Nazism was already fully entrenched in the Reich. The totalitarian state had been fully established by 1937, and it was no longer necessary, nor was it always possible, to distinguish definitely between Party and state organisation.
   (c) While the SA, SS and NSKK only gradually took over functions as auxiliary formations of the regular Armed Forces, the NSFK was, from the outset, intended to

serve as the training and recruiting organisation of the Luftwaffe, which at that time was expanding fast.

2. Development

The actual reason for the late founding of the NSFK may be sought mainly in the foreign policy of the Third Reich in the years immediately following the accession to power of the Nazi Party.

The Nazi Reich Government, from 1933 onward, was eager to impress the outside world, and to camouflage its military preparations. It proclaimed repeatedly that Germany, under its new leadership, fulfilled the demands of the Versailles Treaty to the letter. (One point of this treaty specifically prohibits the support of air-sport from public funds.)

Thus aviation as such remained, at least on the surface, a matter of private initiative. To illustrate, however, to what extent preparations for air expansion were already under way, it should be recalled, that the Lufthansa, semi-official German airways monopoly, evaded the Versailles Treaty by an over-expanded production and training schedule. Its role in the field of aviation corresponded to that of the Black Reichswehr in the field of the transformation of the 100,000 men strong professional army to the present Wehrmacht.

It is, however, certain that German industry, the Reichswehr and virtually all nationalist circles, even during the Weimar Republic, looked with great hopes to the many clubs of model airplane builders, glider sportsmen and similar air-minded private organisations. Generous "assistance" was accorded many of these Vereine.

In 1933, immediately following the accession to power of the Nazi Party, these numerous Segel- und Gleitflugverbände (Leagues for the furtherance of glider aviation) were dissolved. This was mainly done in order to coordinate their activities completely with the new Nazi State and to make them a ready tool in the hands of the sponsors of aviation, the Party Chiefs, and the military.

Following their dissolution, these scattered clubs and leagues of clubs were reorganised and in their totality became the Deutsche Luftsport Verband (DLV or German Aviation Sport League), which was fully controlled by the Party.

The so-called Fliegerstürme (aviation companies) of the SA and SS were also incorporated into the DLV, and took a leading role in its administration. This nazification created a centrally administered organisation which served as the first reserve and training agency for the developing Luftwaffe and was soon to become the NSFK.

3. Primary Functions

From the beginning the primary functions of the NSFK were defined as follows:
(a) Instruction in flying and training of German youth below military age to provide the G.A.F. with a continuous flow of partially trained personnel.
(b) Training and re-training of members of all ages in all technical fields connected with aviation such as maintenance, repair work, radio operation, aeronautics, etc.
(c) Furtherance and fostering of air-mindedness among the German people in general and the young adherents of Nazism in particular.

PART II

TRAINING AND RECRUITING

4. The NSFK and the Hitler Youth

The training of the future German pilot begins when he has reached the age of twelve. The construction of model planes under supervision and with the guidance and assistance of experts, represents the first grade of his pre-military air training. This activity is given considerable publicity in Germany and is regarded as an excellent means of getting the young interested in planes.

Local and national contests are prominently advertised and held under the auspices of popular aces.

It is also believed that the construction of model planes shows at an early stage who among the young trainees are especially interested and adept and are likely to be later selected for service in the air force. The construction of models is partly taught on a volunteer basis and partly as an obligatory subject of instruction in the curriculum of secondary schools and in the Modellfluggruppen (model building groups) of the Deutsches Jungvolk (the junior branch of the Hitler Youth Organisation.)

5. Training with Model Planes

A decree dated 3- December 1939 introduced the construction of model planes as an obligatory subject for all male pupils from the ages of 12 to 13. Article 2 of the decree charges the NSFK with the teaching of this subject in all schools.

In addition, teachers are exhorted to become members of the NSFK and to further the forming of model plane construction groups among the DJ (Deutsches Jungvolk) outside school hours.

German boys receive weekly two hours instruction in model construction. At least once each month, normally on a Sunday, they must attend Pflichtflüge (obligatory flying) and test in the open the models which they have built.

Modellfluglehrer (instructors in model construction) are especially trained at the Reichsmodellflugschulen of the NSFK.

Pimpfe (Junior members of the compulsory Hitler Youth Organisation) who have served their third or fourth year, are organised into DJ-Modellgruppen (Model groups of the junior branch of the Hitler Youth Organisation). Members of these groups, however, are mainly those who have already definitely decided to specialise in the field of aviation, which is to become their later profession. Past experience has proved that a considerable number of German youths have thus been prepared for air force service at the age of 13 and 14. Their greatest experience at that stage is participation in the annual Reichswettkampf, (National Competitive Meet) on the Wasserkuppe.

Although construction of model planes and their testing is primarily confined to younger boys, these activities are by no means neglected by older ones. A special Modellflug-Leistungsgruppe der HJ (Hitler Youth Advanced

Model Aviation Group) comprises all members of the Flieger-HJ (Aviation branch of the Hitler Youth) who have achieved outstanding successes in model construction. (The group is made up of boys aged 14 and over.)

These advanced model builders attend the technische Schulen (technical schools) of the NSFK. Thus the NSFK has succeeded in making model plane construction a truly popular sport. Hochstartgeräte ("High Launching Ramps") have been erected on flat terrain in virtually all regions of Germany to facilitate model testings, and natural slopes serve in hilly or mountainous territories.

The extent to which model flying has developed may be gathered from a report of NSFK-Gruppe 17, rendered in 1943: within this one group command 13,122 models had been constructed; of planes launched by hand and without mechanical power, one glider model set a record by staying in the air while covering a distance of 43 km; the record for petrol driven models was set by one which covered 112 km, the runway start being included in this distance. The report also asserted that model flying time of one hour or more was no longer a rarity.

6. Training in the Flieger-HJ

The future candidate for the Luftwaffe enters the Flieger-Hitlerjugend (Aviation branch of the Hitler Youth Organisation) at the age of 14.

According to directives issued on 21 May 1940, governing the cooperation between the HJ and NSFK, the HJ is charged with the physical training, the ideological and political indoctrination, the target practice and the "gelandedienstlich Ausbildung" (topographical training and terrain intelligence) of the Flieger HJ.

The NSFK is charged with technical and aviation training.

Instruction during the first year covers basic aeronautics including the following subjects: navigation, meteorology, aviation instruments and motors, aviation geography, laws and regulations governing international aviation and air currents. Glider flying and parachute jumping are taught in the second year.

7. Glider Training: Certificates and Badges.

According to the pre-military training programme of the NSFK, boys aged 15 must pass their Segelflug-A-Prüfung (Grade "A" Gliding Examination), those aged 16 must pass their B-Prüfung and those aged 17 their C-Prüfung.

Qualifications for the Segelflieger-Abzeichen "A" ("A" Certificate for Glider Flying) are the following:
Minimum of 30 starts.
Five test flights on a straight-away course, four of which must last not less than 20 seconds each.
The fifth to last at least 30 seconds duration.
All landings must be achieved within a distance of 30 metres on a pre-designated landing area.

The qualification for the "B" Certificate a minimum of 20 flights after the candidate has obtained the "A" certificate, on a curved S-shaped flying course, five of the flights being of not less than 60 seconds duration.

The qualification for the "C" certificate is a minimum of 20 flights after the candidate has obtained the "B" certificate. All these flights must be of at least one minute duration and five of them of not less than two minutes' duration. The total time in the air must amount to not less than 30 minutes.

Both "B" and "C" tests stipulate that all landings must be achieved within an area of 50 x 250 metres.

Other NSFK certificates (and awarded badges) which however are hardly achieved by its younger members, are the following ones:

    a. <u>Segelflieger-Leistungsabzeichen in Silber</u> (Glider achievement badge in silver); awarded after a flight lasting 5 hours with return to the starting point, or after a straight flight covering a distance of 50 km, or after a flight in which an altitude of 1,000 metres has been gained above the starting point.

    b. <u>Segelflieger-Leistungsabzeichen in Gold</u> (Glider Achievement Badge in Gold); awarded to holders of the silver badge, who have made a straight flight over a distance of 300 km, or a flight in which an altitude of 3,000 metres above the starting point has been reached.

    c. <u>Luftfahrschein für Segelflugzeugführer</u> (Aviation Certificate for Glider Pilots); is issued in three grades and awarded to graduate glider operators. Examinations covering theoretical subjects, and <u>Schleppflüge</u> (tow flights) are demanded of candidates for this highest-ranking certificate issued by the NSFK.

8. <u>Further training of the Flieger HJ</u>.

<u>Hitlerjungen</u> (HJ members) who have passed the "C" examination are sent for more advanced training to one of the many <u>Segelflugschulen der NSFK</u> (Glider Schools of the NSFK).

They are under close observation and future crew members of motor-driven planes are selected to enter special courses by the instructors and supervisors of these institutions.

By this process the NSFK not only functions as training agency of future Luftwaffe recruits, but also controls their selection.

Since the outbreak of the war in 1939 the training in motor aviation previously undertaken by the NSFK has been considerably curtailed: most training planes and establishments were directly transferred to the <u>Luftwaffe</u>. Nevertheless, a considerable number of booty planes, above all the French planes of the Model Morane MS 230 were handed over to the NSFK, especially for training purposes, and also as tow planes for NSFK gliders.

It is also of interest that the <u>Nationalpolitische Erziehungsanstalt</u> ("Napola", or national political educational institute) at KÖSLIN, Pomerania, instituted Sonderzüge (Special courses) for the advanced training of officers and graduate engineers of the <u>Luftwaffe</u> under NSFK auspices.

9. **Wireless Training.**

The <u>Flieger-Hitlerjugend</u> is not only given glider training but also receives instruction in other fields. <u>Bordfunk</u> (wireless operation) is being given special attention. A special <u>Bordfunkerschein</u> (Aviator's wireless operator's licence) is issued in accordance with regulations specified by the <u>Luftwaffe</u>, and officers of the GAF supervise examination for this certificate, which generally entitles the holder to be enlisted as special technician in an Air Signal unit when called up for service. As the NSFK, owing to increased wartime demand, was unable to supply an adequate number of wireless instructors, both <u>Luftwaffe</u> and <u>Reichspost</u> (Postal Administration) have supplied the NSFK with instructors.

10. **Workshop Training.**

A considerable number of workshops exist in Germany where boys are being given instructions in repair and maintenance work and where they are familiarised with airplane motors and aeronautical instruments. The future specialists for the ground crews of the <u>Luftwaffe</u> receive their pre-military training in these workshops.

Again, the Directorate of the Reichs Postal Authorities lend its support to these activities, by placing workshops and material at the disposal of the NSFK. A special liaison officer, NSFK Standartenführer THIELE, has been appointed by the Reichsminister for Postal Affairs to assist in the furthering of adequate collaboration between the postal authorities and the NSFK

Note: The Werkstätten (workshops) of the NSFK must not be confused with the Werkstürme des NSFK. The latter are units of company level composed of NSFK members, but organised not according to their residence but to their place of employment, namely industrial plants. (The organisation of these units was facilitated by the fact that increased control is exercised in industrial plants to compel "voluntary membership").

11. **Parachute Training.**

Besides this, members of the <u>Flieger-Hitlerjugend</u> are also trained by the NSFK in the maintenance of parachutes. At the technical schools of the NSFK these boys, aged from 14 to 18 years, undergo basic training, each course lasting several weeks.
Parachutes and their operation are carefully studied in great detail theoretically and practically. Instruction includes "landing in high wind". Finally members of the <u>Flieger-HJ</u> are also trained in the use, repair and maintenance of rubber life-boats.

12. **NSFK Membership.**

Members of the <u>Flieger-HJ</u> are in peace time transferred to the NSFK after they have reached their 18th year. It is likely that such a transfer in wartime is effected at the age of 17, or possibly 16. Although the NSFK has repeatedly stated that it considers it

desirable to limit its membership to former members of
the Flieger-HJ, other volunteers are now accepted
provided they meet the following qualifications:

    a) Unblemished character
    b) Physical fitness (maximum age 45)
    c) Aryan descent ("grosser Nachweis" proving
"pure German ancestry" to the year 1750)
    d) Eligibility and worthiness to become a
a member of the Nazi party according to the latter's
byelaws and regulations:

    Besides this, two other groups are eligible
for membership in the NSFK:
    a) Members of the second reserve of the Luftwaffe.
       (Angehörige des Beurlaubtenstandes)
    b) German citizens (Reichsdeutsche) who are
licensed pilots.

As for the second group it seems that the general
qualifications demanded under (a) to (d) above need not
to be met, as any shortcomings from a Nazi ideological
point of view are "adequately compensated for" by the
"experience and usefulness" of these men.

13. Honorary Membership

Virtually everybody may become a Förderer (sponsoring
patron) of the NSFK. As such he contributes to the fund
of that organisation, a fee ranging from 1 Reichsmark per
month upwards. In this manner all the employees of a
considerable number of large industrial undertakings (such
as airplane plants) have united to form sponsoring patron
groups of the NSFK.

All employees of the German Postal Directorate in
Dresden, Saxony (16,000) have automatically become a group
of Förderer - presumably on a voluntary basis. (Contrib-
utions are directly deductable from pay checks, and such
sponsors are legally entitled to display on their motor
vehicles the NSFK insignia).

14. Changes during the War.

Before the outbreak of war in 1939 the NSFK had
trained 8,000 of the 18,000 trained pilots "at the
disposal of the Luftwaffe". At that time the NSFK
training programme was conducted in 20 Motorflugzeug-
führerschulen (Motor aviation pilot training centres).

By special arrangement with the Luftwaffe a graduate
training certificate was issued to those who had passed
through this institution. The purpose of this document
was to ensure, that upon being called to the colours, its
holders would be regarded as members of Air Force Reserve
I and inducted into the appropriate flying or Air Signal
branch.

Since the outbreak of war these schools, however,
are directly operated by the Luftwaffe. Nevertheless
their staffs consist primarily of old NSFK instructors.

Thus, a clear distinction between Luftwaffe and
NSFK personnel in the reserve and training establishments
of the GAF is no longer possible, e.g. the so-called

Ballonstürme (Balloon companies) of the NSFK were bodily incorporated into the Luftwaffe and today form the nuclei of the crews manning German balloon barrages.

15. **NSFK And The Luftwaffe**

The relations between the G.A.F. and the NSFK may be summed up as follows:

a) The NSFK is subordinated to the Commander of the Luftwaffe (GÖRING)
b) The Korpsführer of the NSFK (Commander-in-Chief) is an active general of the Luftwaffe.
c) The technical training and all subsequent examinations and tests of the NSFK are planned, supervised and to a large extent conducted by officers of the Luftwaffe. Conversely, NSFK officers also supervise training in and serve as instructors in centres and schools operated by the GAF.
d) The NSFK submits to the appropriate Wehrmeldeamt (Local Military Recruiting and Registration Office) lists giving home addresses of all members of the HJ who have been transferred to the NSFK.
e) Each NSFK Group Command appoints a Verbindungsführer (liaison officer) to the Wehrersatzinspektion (Military sub-district of the Wehrmacht) in its territory.
f) The certificates issued by the NSFK entitle holders to induction into special branches of the Air Force once they are called up for military service.
g) Pilot schools of the NSFK have been turned over to the Luftwaffe in their entirety.
h) The balloon companies of the NSFK have been bodily incorporated into the barrage units of the Luftwaffe.

PART III

ORGANISATION AND STRENGTH

16. Group Organisation

The NSFK is organised on a territorial basis. Germany is for this purpose divided into 18 NSFK-Gruppen (Group Commands).

These regions comprise generally from 1 to 3 NSDAP-Gaue (Party Districts), the borders coinciding exactly with the boundaries of the Party regions. Only in one case is a Party District split up and allotted to several NSFK-Gruppen.

Inasmuch as Party Gaue are identical with the Reichsverteidigungsbezirke (Reich Defence Regions) it is noteworthy that the NS Aviation Corps is the only Party sponsored formation in which the regional organisation completely follows Party lines. (Some of the boundaries of NSFK group commands do, however, coincide with those of the Luftgaue, the administrative districts of the GAF.)

NSFK-Gruppen are designated by consecutive Arabic numerals from 1 to 18 but also bear such geographical names as OSTLAND, NORDWEST, WESER-EIBE or SCHWABEN. (It is noteworthy that the names of NSFK-Gruppen, in several cases, do not define regions by the same name in such formations as the RAD or SA.)

17. Organisation: Standarten and Below

Each NSFK group is organised into from 3 to 7 Standarten (Regiments). Eighty-one Standarten have probably been identified.

These bear Arabic numerals in the series from 1 to 201. It appears that regimental numbers are allotted in series to NSFK-Gruppen (e.g. 8 to 12, to Gruppe OSTSEE).

The minimum peace time strength of a Standarte is generally 1,500 officers and men.

Each NSFK regiment is organised into 10 - 12 Stürme (Companies); one Standarte is believed to contain 18 Stürme.

Each Sturm covers normally a territory equivalent to a Landkreis or Stadtkreis (Rural or Urban Governmental Administrative Sub-District).

The peace time strength of a Sturm is normally 120 men.

Each Sturm is organised into 3 Trupps (Platoons), and each Trupp into 3 Scharen (Sections), the latter having about 12 men.

It is of interest that the NSFK does not organise its Stürme into Sturmbanne (Battalions) and its Standarten into Brigaden as do such formations as the SS, SA and NSKK. These intermediate units are obviously omitted because the NS Aviation Corps is primarily a training organisation, its units never having been committed to any action or activity as formations. Another reason may be the fact that the NSFK is numerically one of the smallest para-military forces of Germany.

18. **NSFK Commanders**

The first Korpsführer (Commander-in-Chief) of the NSFK, appointed 1937, was General der Flieger Friedrich CHRISTIANSEN, until recently the Wehrmachtsbefehlshaber (Armed Forces' Commander) in the Netherlands.

CHRISTIANSEN, originally in the Merchant Marine, was a combat aviator in the German Navy during the last War, credited with 14 air victories. He received the highest decoration of Imperial Germany, namely, the Pour le Merite. After World War I he served in the Lufthansa as Captain of the Dirigible DOX.

His successor, the present Korpsführer since 1943, is Generaloberst Alfred KELLER (62), a career officer. In 1918 he was a captain and until 1943 Chief of a German Air Fleet. He has no Party background. The appointment of an active General Officer without known Party affiliation may be indicative that the purely military control over the NSFK, at least until recently, has progressively increased.

The Korpsführer is assisted by a staff of NSFK officers, headed by the "Vertreter des Korpsführers und Chef des Stabes" (Permanent Acting Deputy of the Commander-in-Chief and Chief-of-Staff). At present the post is filled by NSFK-Obergruppenführer Karl SAUKE (47). He served throughout World War I in the Imperial German Forces, joined the Nazi Party in 1929, and was appointed to his present rank in 1937. According to a PW report of Feb 45 the CoS is Gruf Karl BRINKMANN

19. **NSFK High Command HQ**

The NSFK-Korpsführung (High Command), located at Berlin W.15, Meier-Otto-Strasse 8-9, is organised into ten Abteilungen (Sections). The heads of these Sections are directly responsible to SAUKE; the Chef des Verwaltungsamtes (Chief of the Administrative Bureau) heading an eleventh sub-division (Amt) is directly responsible to KELLER. Details follow:-

Führungsamt (Operational HQ)	BF. Arno KEHRBERG
Abteilung I : Segelflug (Gliding Aviation)	OF. KUNZ
Abteilung II : Modellflug (Model Aviation)	SF. BENGSCH
Abteilung III : Technik (Technical)	SF. Max EICHHORN
Abteilung IV : Motor and Ballon	SF. THOMSEN
Abteilung V : Wehrsport und Weltanschauung (Military Sports Training and Indoctrination)	SF. IEDY
Abteilung VI Personal	BF. BASTGEN

<u>Abteilung VII</u> :
   <u>Film, Bild, Unterricht</u>
   (Film, Propaganda and Instruction)

<u>Abteilung VIII</u>:
   <u>Sanitätswesen</u> (Medical Services)

<u>Abteilung IX</u> :
   <u>Rechtswesen</u> (Jurisdictional and Legal)

The <u>Verwaltungsamt</u> (VA; Administrative Bureau) is divided into 9 sub-sections, all but one of them designated V.A. 1 to V.A. 8. They are:

V.A. 1   <u>Haushalt und Organization</u>
   (Budget and Organisation)

V.A. 2   <u>Revision</u>
   (Auditing Control)

V.A. 3   <u>Kassen- und Rechnungswesen</u>
   (Financial Affairs and Accounts)

V.A. 4   <u>Besoldungswesen und Reisekosten</u>
   (Pay and Travel Expenditures)

V.A. 5   <u>Unterkunft und Gerät</u>
   (Quarters and Equipment)

V.A. 6   <u>Bauwesen</u>
   (Building Constructions)

V.A. 7   <u>Bekleidung, Ausrüstung, Verpflegung</u>
   (Clothing, Personal Equipment, and Rations)

V.A. 8   <u>Versicherungswesen</u>
   (Insurance matters)

- - -   <u>Beschaffungsstelle</u>
   (Acquisition, "Procurement")

20. Schools and Training Centres

The following schools and training centres are operated by the NSFK. The Arabic numerals listed in brackets after each school indicate the region of the Group Command in which these schools are located. This does not, however, mean that all listed schools are controlled directly by Group Command HQ, as some may be under the immediate control of the NSFK High Command. The Order of Battle (ANNEXE A) following this text lists under each <u>NSFK-Gruppe</u> such schools and training establishments definitely known as controlled by the Group Command HQ in question.

FLUGZEUGFÜHRERSCHULEN: (Pilot Schools)	
Tilsit	(1)
Allenstein	(1)
Königsberg	(1)
Schönfeld	(2)
Hamburg-Fulsbüttel	(3)
Breslau-Gandau	(6)
Dresden-Heller	(7)

CONFIDENTIAL

19. **NSFK High Command HQ**

The general organisation of the NSKK Korpsführung (High Command HQ) is contained in the revised diagram given in Annexe B, which is based on the Organisationsbuch der NSDAP, 1943.

In addition to his ständiger bevollmächtigter Vertreter des Korpsführers und Chef des Stabes (Permanent Acting Deputy of the Commander-in-Chief and Chief of Staff) the Korpsführer has as his immediate assistants the following officials:-

    The Inspekteur (Inspector), who supervises activity in schools and training establishments
    The Adjutant
    The z.b.V. (Personnel for special duties).

The NSFK-Korpsführung (HQ) located at Berlin W 15, Meier-Otto-Strasse 8-9 is organised into five Ämter (Bureaux):-

    Führungsamt (Operational HQ)
    Personalamt (Personnel)
    Ausbildungsamt (Training)
    Verwaltungsamt (Administration)
    Sanitätsamt (Medical).

Each Amt is headed by an Amtschef (Chief) who is directly responsible to the Chef des Stabes. The Ämter are sub-divided into:-

    Fachabteilungen (Specialised Departments)
    Hauptreferate (Main Sections)
    Referate (Sections).

The following breakdown of the three main Ämter is taken from a German document, dated 1940 and may therefore, in some instances, be out of date (cf. Annexe B, and Note below).

The FÜHRUNGSAMT (F.A. - Operational HQ) under HF. Arno KEHRBERG, is divided into the following sections:-

O.- Organisation	(Organisation)
* P.- Personal	(Personnel)
Pr.- Presse und Propaganda	(Press and Propaganda)
F.- Film- und Bildlehrmittel	(Film and Visual aid in Propaganda)
G.- Gefolgschaftsbetreuung	(Personnel Welfare)

The AUSBILDUNGSAMT (Ab.A.- Bureau for Training), which controls the Amt Nationaler Luftsport (Bureau of National "Aviation Sport"), is divided into the following sections:-

I - Segelflug	(Gliding Aviation)
OF. KUNZ	
II - Modellflug	(Model Aviation)
SF. BENGSCH	
III - Motorflug und Ballonsport	
SF. THOMSEN	
IV - Technik	(Technical)
SF. Max EICHHORN	
V - Wehrsport, Sport und Weltanschauliche Schulung	(Military Sports, Sports, and Indoctrination)
SF. LEDY	
VI - Unterricht und Funkausbildung	(Wireless Instruction and Training)

* Presumably this section of the Führungsamt has now become the Personalamt (which did not exist in the 1940 organisation).

(E.D.S./G/2, Amendment No. 3 of Apr 1945)

CONFIDENTIAL

(revised para 19, contd.)

The VERWALTUNGSAMT (V.A.- Administrative Bureau), divided into the following sections:-

V.A.1 - Haushalt, Organisation		(Budget and Organisation)
V.A.2 - Revision		(Auditing Control)
V.A.3 - Kassenwesen		(Financial Affairs)
V.A.4 - Besoldung, Reisekosten, Umzüge		(Pay, Travelling Expenses, Removals)
V.A.5 - Liegenschaften		(Real Estates)
V.A.6 - Bauwesen		(Building Constructions)
V.A.7 - Bekleidung, Ausrüstung, Verpflegung		(Clothing, Personal Equipment, Rations)
V.A.8 - Versicherung		(Insurance)
V.A.9 - Rechtswesen		
Prüfstelle 1) Prüfstelle 2)		(Sections for "checking")

Beschaffungsstelle: Berlin S.W.29, Hasenheide 5/6

The 1940 document also lists (in the form of an amendment) under the NSFK Korpsführung, a Nachschubstelle (supply depot) at Worms am Rhein, Flughafen.

NOTE: According to latest information, a PW Report (dated 14 Feb 45) gives the following information, considered reliable by the interrogator, which supplements the above breakdown of the NSFK Headquarters and its functions.

The Führungsamt, headed by OF KELLNER (not KEHRBERG) has been officially discontinued. Chief of section Organisation was Staf. Franz von PUSCH who was also chief of section Förderwesen (Promotions) formerly section Personal. Chief of section Presse und Propaganda was Stubaf. Alfred JUHRE. Section Film- und Bildlehrmittel was apparently headed by a woman.
Chief of the Personalamt is Gruf. FRODIEN.
OF. Joseph KUNZ is chief of the Ausbildungsamt; section II Segelflug operates under his personal direction. Section Motorflug und Ballonsport has ceased to function. Staf. Walter HILLERSCHEID is responsible for Weltanschauliche Schulung. Ostubaf. PITSCHELT is chief of section Unterricht und Funkausbildung.
Chief of the Verwaltungsamt is OF. Willmar KOEPPNER. Section VA-I (combination of former VA 1, 2, 3) is headed by Stubaf. LETHNER. Section VA-II (combination of former VA 5, 6, 7 and Beschaffungsstelle) has as its chief Stubaf. Karl SEEBECK. Section VA-III (same as former VA 8) is headed by OF. Dr. DOEHRING and Section VA-IV (same as former VA 4) by Staf. HINZ.

(E.D.S./G/2, Amendment No. 3 of Apr 1945)

CONFIDENTIAL

20. Schools and Training Centres

Information derived from a captured document ("Anschriften Verzeichnis des NS-Fliegerkorps", dated 1940) and a PW Report, dated 14 Feb 45 have made it possible to add further details to the list of NSFK Schools and training establishments given in the original paragraph 20 of this publication.

The PW Report states that on the whole the curriculum has been curtailed. Glider, elementary signals and navigation are the main subjects. The schools operate the year round. Each course lasts 4 - 6 weeks, and 60 - 80 students are enrolled. An exception is Trebbin, where advanced training for instructors is conducted.

It has been found necessary to set out a new list below including the two new sources of information, owing to the fact that the original list was compiled from various sources and the "Anschriften Verzeichnis" (referred to in the list below as "1940 Document") contains a number of undated amendments made by the Germans. Wherever the information conflicts the alternatives have been given and their source mentioned.

According to PW Report all Flugzeugführerschulen (Pilot Schools) were turned over to the GAF some time ago. In the 1940 Document a number of Flugzeugführerschulen (M) are mentioned; exact meaning of the "(M)" is not known. According to the PW, the following changes have taken place.

Technische Schulen (Technical Schools) formerly designated Werkstattleiterschulen (Workshop Instructors Schools) are now closed with the exception of two (see list), while of the Segelflugbauschulen (Glider Construction Schools) all but one, possibly two, have been closed. All Reichsschulen für Motorflugsport (National Schools for Motor Aviation Sports) have been closed. With the exception of Fischbeck/Hamburg all Segelflugschulen (Glider Schools) are still operating. Modellflugschulen (Model Schools) are also still functioning.

LOCATION	GRUPPE	TYPE OF SCHOOL	REMARKS
Aigen	17	Flugzeugführerschule (M)	
Allenstein	1	Flugzeugführerschule	
Altona	3	Reichsschule für Motorflugsport	
Ballenstedt	9	Segelflugschule	
Bielefeld	10	Flugzeugführerschule	
Borkenberge	10	Segelflugschule	
Braunschweig	9	Flugzeugführerschule	
Breslau-Gandau	6	Flugzeugführerschule	
Bunzlau	6	Modellflugschule	
Chemnitz	7	Reichsschule für Motorflugsport or Reichsschule für Motorflug	According to 1940 Document
Danzig-Langfuhr	Brig.125	Flugzeugführerschule	For former Brig.125, see Annexe A, Gruppe 18
Deuthen b. Allenstein	1	Werkstattleiterschule	
Dinkelsbühl	13	Werkstattleiterschule	Still operating according to PW Report
Dörnberg	8	Segelflugschule	
Dresden-Heller	7	Flugzeugführerschule	
Erfurt	8	Flugzeugführerschule	
Esslingen	15	Segelflugbauschule or Technische Schule	According to PW Report According to 1940 Document

(E.D.S./G/2, Amendment No. 3 of Apr 1945)

CONFIDENTIAL

(revised para 20, contd.)

LOCATION	GRUPPE	TYPE OF SCHOOL	REMARKS
Fischbeck/Hamburg	3	Segelflugschule	
Fischbeck/Harburg	3	Segelflugschule	Deleted in 1940 Document
Frankfurt-Rebstock	11	Flugzeugführerschule	
Freiburg	16	Flugzeugführerschule	
Fürstenberg/Oder	4	Segelflugbauschule or Technische Schule	According to PW Report. According to PW Report formerly Segelflugbauschule and now still operating as Technische Schule
Gandau	6	Reichsflugschule	Closed according to PW Report
Gelsenkirchen	10	Flugzeugführerschule	
Gmunden	17	Modellflugschule	
Grossrückerswalde	7	Segelflugschule	
Hamburg-Fuhlsbüttel	3	Flugzeugführerschule	Deleted in 1940 Document
Hamburg-Holstenhof	3	Segelflugbauschule	Closed according to PW Report
Hamburg-Wandsbeck	3	Segelflugbauschule or Technische Schule	According to 1940 Document
Hannover	9	Werkstattleiterschule (Technische Schule des NSFK)	
Harsberg	8	Segelflugschule	
Hesselberg	13	Segelflugschule	
Hoher Meissner	8	Modellflugschule or Flugmodellbauschule or Reichsmodellflugschule	Deleted in 1940 Document. Correction in 1940 Document
Hornberg/Württemberg	15	Reichsschule für Segelflugsport or Reichssegelflugschule	According to PW Report
Hummerich	11	Segelflugschule	
Ith	9	Reichssegelflugschule	
Kamenz	7	Segelflugbauschule	According to PW Report possibly still operating
Karlsruhe/Baden	16	Reichsschule für Motorflugsport or Flugzeugführerschule	According to 1940 Document
Köln	12	Reichsschule für Motorflugsport or Flugzeugführerschule	According to 1940 Document
Königsberg	1	Flugzeugführerschule	
Laucha	7	Segelflugschule	

(E.D.S./G/2, Amendment No. 3 of Apr 1945)

CONFIDENTIAL

(revised para 20, contd.)

LOCATION	GRUPPE	TYPE OF SCHOOL	REMARKS
Lauenburg	3	Modellflugschule or Flugmodellbauschule or Reichsmodellflugschule	Deleted in 1940 Document Correction in 1940 Document
Mannheim	16	Flugzeugführerschule	
München-Gladbach	12	Flugzeugführerschule or Flugzeugführerschule (M)	According to 1940 Document
Rangsdorf	4	Reichsschule für Motorflugsport	
Regensburg	13	Flugzeugführerschule	
Rehme	10	Technische Schule	According to 1940 Document
Rhinow	4	Segelflugschule	
Rossgarten	6	Wehrsportschule	Closed according to PW Report. 1940 Document records as belonging to Gruppe 5.
Rossitten	1	Segelflugschule or Reichssegelflugschule	According to 1940 Document
Rothenburg ob der Tauber	14	Modellflugschule or Reichsmodellflugschule	1943 Source
Salzgitter	9	Segelflugschule	Formerly Gitter am Berge
Schönfeld	2	Flugzeugführerschule or Motorflugzeugführerschule	According to 1940 Document
Schüren	10	Segelflugschule	
Schwangau	14	Segelflugschule	
Sensburg	1	Segelflugschule	
Spitzerberg	17	Segelflugschule or Reichssegelflugschule	According to 1940 Document
Sonthofen	14	Flugzeugführerschule or Motorflugzeugführerschule	According to 1940 Document
Steinberg	6	Segelflugschule	
Teck	15	Segelflugschule	
Tilsit	1	Flugzeugführerschule	
Trebbin	4	Segelflugschule	
Trebbin	4	Erprobungsstelle	According to PW Report formerly Versuchsstelle; used only as a resting ground for gliders and glider equipment

(E.D.S./G/2, Amendment No. 3 of Apr 1945)

(revised para 20, contd.)

LOCATION	GRUPPE	TYPE OF SCHOOL	REMARKS
Vogelsang	12	Flugzeugführerschule or Motorflugzeugführerschule	According to 1940 Document
Wasserkuppe	8	Segelflugschule or Reichssegelflugschule	According to 1940 Document
Zell am See	17	Segelflugschule or Hochalpine Segelflugschule	According to 1940 Document

(revised para 20, contd.)

(E.D.S./G/2, Amendment No. 3 of Apr 1945)

FLUGZEUGFÜHRERSCHULEN: (continued)	Erfurt	(8)
	Braunschweig	(9)
	Gelsenkirchen-Buer	(10)
	Bielefeld	(10)
	Frankfurt-Rebstock	(11)
	München-Gladbach	(12)
	Vogelsang	(12)
	Regensburg	(13)
	Sonthofen	(14)
	Freiburg	(16)
	Mannheim	(16)
	Aigen	(17)
WERKSTATTLEITERSCHULEN: (Workshop Instructors' School)	Deuthen b. Allenstein	(1)
	Hannover (Techn. Schule des NSFK)	(9)
	Schüren b. Meschede	(10)
	Dinkelsbühl	(13)
SEGELFLUGBAUSCHULEN: (Glider Construction Schools)	Hamburg-Wandsbeck, Holstenhof	(3)
	Fürstenberg/O	(4)
	Kamenz	(7)
	Esslingen	(15)
REICHSSCHULEN FÜR MOTORFLUGSPORT: (National Schools for Motor Aviation Sports)	Altona	(3)
	Rangsdorf	(4)
	Chemnitz	(7)
	Köln	(12)
	Karlsruhe	(16)
REICHSSCHULE FÜR SEGELFLUGSPORT: (National School for Glider Sports)	Hornberg	(15)
REICHSFLUGSCHULE: (National School of Aviation)	Gandau	(6)
WEHRSPORTSCHULE DES NSFK: (Military Sports Training Centre)	Rossgarten	(6)
VERSUCHSSTELLE DES NSFK: (Experimental Station)	Trebbin	(4)
SEGELFLUGSCHULEN: (Glider Schools)	Rossitten	(1)
	Sensburg	(1)
	Fischbeck	(3)
	Trebbin	(4)
	Rhinow	(4)
	Steinberg	(6)
	Grossrückerswalde	(7)
	Laucha	(7)
	Dörnberg	(8)
	Harsberg (8)	
	Wasserkuppe	(8)
	Ballenstedt	(9)

SEGELFLUGSCHULEN: (continued)	Salzgitter	(9)
	Borkenberge	(10)
	Schüren	(10)
	Hummerich	(11)
	Hesselberg	(13)
	Schwangau	(14)
	Teck	(15)
	Spitzergerb	(17)
	Zell am See	(17)
MODELLFLUGSCHULEN: (Model Schools)	Lauenberg	(3)
	Bunzlau	(6)
	Hoher Meissner	(8)
	Rothenburg ob der Tauber	(14)
	Gmunden	(17)

21. Strength

The last official report of the total strength of the NSFK as issued in 1938 states that this Corps has a total membership of 62,000 regular members (the NSFK counting at that time only 15 group commands totalling approximately 60 Standarten). To this must be added 76,000 members of the Flieger-HJ who came directly under the jurisdiction of the NSFK and 350,000 sponsoring patrons.

Over 100,000 Pimpfe (See para 4) aged 12 to 14 were organised in the numerous Modellflug-Gruppen (Model Building Groups) of the Deutsches Jungvolk and were also in their specialised activity directly under the supervision of the NSFK.

The present strength of active NSFK members including its junior members in the Hitler Youth is estimated at around 300,000, of which, however, two thirds are believed to serve today in the GAF.

PART IV

UNIFORMS AND RANKS

22. Uniforms

The traditional uniform of the NSFK is not unlike that of the SA. Normally the brown shirt is worn with grey breeches and black boots, the trousers being of the same material as that worn by members of the Luftwaffe. An air force grey tunic may also be worn. The tie is black.

The insignia of the NSFK (a wing-spreading Icarus over a swastika and the abbreviation N.S.F.K. above) is worn on the right breast, usually as metal clasp.

A Sam Browne belt is worn formally with the broad-handled NSFK dagger.

The regular swastika arm band in black, white circle over red, is worn on the left upper arm.

The cap is shaped like that of the SA (similar to a peaked Norwegian mountain cap) but is made of grey material with yellow piping.

Rank insignia (pips and stripes like those of the SA) are worn on the right collar patch, abbreviated on the left one. (2/15 defining e.g. the 2nd Sturm or company of the 15th Standarte or regiment.)

A Gothic "K" indicates staff members of the Korpsführung (NSFK High Command).

Collar patches are grey with yellow pipings.

The number of the NSFK-Gruppe (Group Command) to which a member belongs is worn on the one shoulder strap, (as in the case of the SA only one shoulder strap is worn on the right side).

In the field, but also at times in Germany proper, the standard German Hoheitsabzeichen (National Emblem) is worn on the left upper arm similar to the one worn by the Waffen-SS, only in its Luftwaffe version (flying eagle clasping a swastika).

Members of NSFK Group Commands covering the Alpine regions wear a metal Edelweiss on the left brim of their cap.

Holders of the Funkschein (Wireless Operators Certificate) wear the Bordfunkerabzeichen (Wireless Operators Badge), a red lightning flash on the left lower arm.

23. Ranks and Insignia

The rank designations and insignia are identical with those of the SA.

NSFK-RANK	WEHRMACHT APPROXIMATION	ABBREVIATION	INSIGNIA ON COLLAR PATCH
1 Mann	Grenadier	None	None
2 Sturmmann	Obergrenadier	Strm	1 vertical stripe
3 Rottenführer	Obergefreiter	Rotf.	2 vertical double stripes

NSFK-RANK	WEHRMACHT APPROXIMATION	ABBREVIATION	INSIGNIA ON COLLAR PATCH
4 Schar-führer	Uffz	Scharf or Schaf	1 pip
5 Oberschar-führer	Unterfeldwebel	Oschaf	1 pip and 1 double stripe
6 Truppführer	Feldwebel	Truppf	2 pips
7 Obertrupp-führer	Oberfeldwebel	OTruppf	2 pips and 1 double stripe
8 Sturm-führer	Lt	Stuf	3 pips
9 Obersturm-führer	Oberleutnant	Ostuf	3 pips and 1 double stripe
10 Hauptsturm-führer (formerly Sturmhauptführer)	Hauptm	Hstuf	3 pips and 2 double stripes
11 Sturmbann-führer	Maj	Stubaf or SBF	4 pips
12 Obersturm-bannführer	Obstlt	Ostubaf or OSBF	4 pips and 1 double stripe
13 Standart-enführer	Obst	Staf or SF	1 oak leaf on each collar patch
14 Oberführer	Obst (Sr.Gr.)	OF or Ofü	2 oak leaves on each collar patch
15 Brigade-führer	Gen. Maj.	Brgf or Brigfü or BF	2 oak leaves and 1 pip on each collar patch
16 Gruppen-führer	Gen. Lt.	Gruf or Grufü or GF	3 oak leaves on each collar patch
17 Obergrup-penführer	Gen.d.Inf.	Ogruf or OGF	3 oak leaves and 1 pip on each collar patch

NSFK-RANK	WEHRMACHT APPROXIMATION	ABBREVIATION	INSIGNIA ON COLLAR PATCH
18 Korpsführer	Gen. Fldm.	Korpsfü	Wreath with NSFK insignia pointing outward in gold on both collar patches

NOTE: All NSFK senior officers from the NSFK-SF upward wear the identical insignia of rank on both the right and left collar patch.

Ranks from 1 - 3 inclusive are termed Mannschaften (OR's); from 4 - 7 NSFK-Unterführer (NCO's); from 8 - 10 Untere Führer (Lesser Commanders or Company Officers); from 11 - 13 Mittlere Führer (Intermediate Commanders or Senior Officers) and from 14 upward Höhere Führer (Superior Commanders or General Officers).

The NSFK ranks and abbreviations in the foregoing table should be prefixed by the letters NSFK in each case.

ANNEXE A.

(Order of Battle Tables)

KEY:

PART ONE: NSFK GRUPPEN

1. "TERRITORY": The NSFK Gruppen are defined under this heading in terms of the Parteigau or Parteigaue with which they are identical.

As the boundaries of NSFK Gruppen have followed the Party Gau boundaries in all cases, no other definitions, e.g., in terms of Wehrkreise, have been made.

2. "COMMAND": Here such details as are available of the last identified Führer (CO), Stellvertretender Führer (Deputy CO), and Stabsführer (Chief of Staff), of the Gruppe are listed.

3. "SCHOOLS": Training centres definitely known to be controlled by the Gruppe are listed.

PART TWO: NSFK STANDARTEN

4. "HQ LOCATION": In quotation marks under the HQ location is given the honorary name of the Standarte, where applicable.

5. "COMPONENT UNITS": Identified Stürme of the Standarte are listed with their HQ locations.

NOTE: German terms and standard abbreviations have been used throughout in order to avoid misinterpretation. Annexe A should be compared throughout with Annexe E

ANNEXE A

NSFK ORDER OF BATTLE

PART ONE: THE NSFK GRUPPEN

Note: Certain NSFK Gruppen have recently been amalgamated for administrative purposes (e.g. Gr. 2 and Gr. 4, jointly designated 2/4). In such cases the former H.Q. of each Gruppe is given below, since the location of the combined H.Q. is not known. With one exception (Gr. 18, now absorbed into Gr. 5) the territory and component Standarten of the individual Gruppen are not affected.

1 - GRUPPE OSTLAND +

TERRITORY (Parteigau):	Ostpreussen
HQ:	KÖNIGSBERG/Pr., Gen.Litzmannstr. 21/25
COMMAND:	OGF. OPPERMANN GoS OF BOLTENHABEN
COMPONENT STANDARTEN:	1 2 3
SCHOOLS CONTROLLED BY GRUPPE:	Flugzeugführerschule Tilsit " Allenstein " Königsberg Segelflugschule Rossitten " Sensburg

2 (2/4) - GRUPPE OSTSEE
(Administratively combined with 4 - Gruppe Berlin-Brandenburg)

TERRITORY (Parteigau):	Mecklenburg, Pommern
HQ:	STETTIN, Arndtstr. 28

COMMAND:
(Gruppen 2 and 4)
	GF. Friedrich Wilhelm FRODIEN
	OF. NAUJOKS (formerly Gr. 2)
	            Stellv.Führer
	OF. GRAMBOW (formerly Gr. 4)
	            Stabsführer

COMPONENT STANDARTEN:	8 9 10 11 12 129
SCHOOLS CONTROLLED BY GRUPPE:	Flugzeugführerschule Schönfeld

3 (3/9) - GRUPPE NORDWEST
(Administratively combined with 9 - Gruppe Weser-Elbe)

TERRITORY (Parteigau):	Hamburg, Schleswig-Holstein, Weser-Ems, Ost-Hannover
	HAMBURG 13, Odenfelderstr. 17
COMMAND: (Gruppen 3 and 9)	GF. Dr. Erwin KRATZ (formerly Gr. 9) OF. REINHOLD (formerly Gr. 3) Stellv.Führer SF. WOLF (formerly Gr. 9) Stabsführer
COMPONENT STANDARTEN:	15 16 17 18

+ According to the 1943 Organisationsbuch der NSDAP, NSFK Gruppe 1 is known as 'Ostpreussen'. A PW report of 1945 states that Gruppen 1 and 18 have been administratively combined.

SCHOOLS CONTROLLED BY GRUPPE:	Flugzeugführerschule Hamburg-Fuhlsbüttel
	Segelflugbauschule Hamburg-Wandsbeck
	Flugmodellbauschule Lauenburg
	Segelflugschule Fischbeck

4 (2/4) BERLIN - BRANDENBURG
(Administratively combined with 2 - Gruppe Ostsee)

TERRITORY (Parteigau):	Berlin, Mark Brandenburg
HQ:	BERLIN, Meier-Otto-Str. 8/9
COMMAND: (Gruppen 2 and 4)	GF. Friedrich Wilhelm FRODIEN
	OF. NAUJOKS (formerly Gr. 2) Stellv.Führer
	OF. GRAMBOW (formerly Gr. 4) Stabsführer
COMPONENT STANDARTEN:	22 23 24 25 26 27
SCHOOLS CONTROLLED BY GRUPPE:	Flugzeugführerschule Rangsdorf
	Segelflugbauschule Fürstenberg/Oder
	Segelflugschule Trebbin
	" Rhinow

5 - WARTHELAND
(Has absorbed former 18 - Gruppe Weichselland)

TERRITORY (Parteigau):	Wartheland (Note: this district has been extended by inclusion of the NSFK units in the General Gouvernement), Danzig-Westpreussen
HQ:	? POSEN, Tiergartenstr. 6 (Note: HQ of former Gruppe 18 was at Danzig, Schichaug. 6)
COMMAND:	GF. Arno KEHRBERG
	CoS OF KREBLITZ
COMPONENT STANDARTEN:	4 119 120 121 125 126
SCHOOLS CONTROLLED BY GRUPPE:	Wehrsportschule Rossgarten

6 - SCHLESIEN

TERRITORY (Parteigau):	Niederschlesien, Oberschlesien
HQ:	BRESLAU, Hindenburgpl. 4
COMMAND:	GF. Gerhard SPORLEDER or
	GF. Friedrich Georg BRINKMANN
	CoS OF GODBERSEN
COMPONENT STANDARTEN:	29 30 31 32 33 34 35
SCHOOLS CONTROLLED BY GRUPPE:	Flugzeugführerschule Breslau-Gandau
	Segelflugschule Steinberg
	Flugmodellbauschule Bunzlau
	Segelfluglager Schwientochlowitz
	Reichsschule für Segelflugsport Hirschberg

7 - ELBE - SAALE

TERRITORY (Parteigau): Halle-Merseburg, Sachsen, Western part of Sudetenland

HQ: DRESDEN - A, Kreutzerstr. 21

COMMAND: GF. Dr. A. ZIMMERMANN
CoS Staf POPP

COMPONENT STANDARTEN: 36 37 38 39 40

SCHOOLS CONTROLLED BY GRUPPE:
Flugzeugführerschule Dresden-Heller
" Chemnitz
Segelflugbauschule Kamenz
Segelflugschule Laucha
" Grossbrückerswalde
" Marienburg-Sachsen

8 - MITTE

TERRITORY (Parteigau): Kurhessen, Thüringen

HQ: ESCHWEGE, Niederhonerstr. 44

COMMAND: **OGF Elmar Frhr von ESCHWEGE**

COMPONENT STANDARTEN: 43 44 45

SCHOOLS CONTROLLED BY GRUPPE:
Flugzeugführerschule Erfurt
Segelflugschule Wasserkuppe
" Harsberg
" Dornberg
Flugmodellbauschule Meissner

9 (3/9) - WESER - ELBE
(Administratively combined with 3 - Gruppe Nordwest)

TERRITORY (Parteigau): Magdeburg-Anhalt, Süd-Hannover-Braunschweig

HQ: HANNOVER, Walderseestr. 1

COMMAND:
(Gruppen 3 and 9)
GF. Dr. Erwin KRATZ (formerly Gr. 9)
OF. REINHOLD (formerly Gr. 3) Stellv. Führer
SF. WOLF (formerly Gr. 9) Stabsführer

COMPONENT STANDARTEN: 50 52 53 55 ?60 ?61 *

SCHOOLS CONTROLLED BY GRUPPE:
Flugzeugführerschule Braunschweig
Segelflugschule Ith
" Gitter
" Ballenstedt
Technische Schule Hannover

*Note: Standarten 60 and 61 were formerly believed to be included in Gruppe 10. Recent information indicates that they form part of Gruppe 9.

10 - WESTFALEN

TERRITORY (Parteigau):	Westfalen-Nord, Westfalen-Süd
HQ:	ÖRLINGHAUSEN in Lippe
COMMAND:	GF. SIELER
	CoS Staf HEIDTMANB
COMPONENT STANDARTEN:	57 58 59 ?60 ?61 * 70
SCHOOLS CONTROLLED BY GRUPPE:	Flugzeugführerschule Gelsenkirchen-Buer
	" Bielefeld
	Segelflugschule Schüren
	" Borkenberge

11 (11/12) - MOSELLAND - HESSEN - WESTMARK
(Administratively combined with 12 - Gruppe Niederrhein)

TERRITORY (Parteigau):	Moselland, Hessen-Nassau
HQ:	FRANKFURT/M., Fellnerstr. 5
COMMAND:	BF. Walter GODT (formerly Gr. 12)
	Stubaf. Alfred BEINES Stabsführer
	CoS Staf WEICHELT
COMPONENT STANDARTEN:	72 75 77 78
SCHOOLS CONTROLLED BY GRUPPE:	Flugzeugführerschule Frankfurt-Rebstock
	Segelflugschule Hummerich
	Segelfluglager Hirzenhain (Dillkr.)

12 (11/12) - NIEDERRHEIN
(Administratively combined with 11 - Gruppe Moselland-Hessen-Westmark)

TERRITORY (Parteigau):	Essen, Düsseldorf, Köln-Aachen
HQ:	ESSEN, Alfredstr. 61/63
COMMAND: (Gruppen 11 and 12)	BF. Walter GODT (formerly Gr. 12)
COMPONENT STANDARTEN:	65 66 67
SCHOOLS CONTROLLED BY GRUPPE:	Flugzeugführerschule München-Gladbach
	" Vogelsang,
	Köln/Rhein

*Note: Standarten 60 and 61 were formerly believed to be included in Gruppe 10. Recent information indicates that they form part of Gruppe 9.

13 - MAIN - DONAU
(May be administratively combined with 14 - Gruppe Hochland)

TERRITORY (Parteigau):	Bayr. Ostmark, Franken, Mainfranken, Sudetenland (South-western part)
HQ:	NÜRNBERG O, Theodorstr. 1
COMMAND:	GF. Carl GRONEISS, Führer OF. Ing. Georg GROHER, Stabsführer
COMPONENT STANDARTEN:	87 88 89 90 91
SCHOOLS CONTROLLED BY GRUPPE:	Flugzeugführerschule Regensburg Werkstattleiterschule Dinkelsbühl Flugmodellbauschule Rothenburg O. Tauber Segelflugschule Hesselberg

14 - HOCHLAND (or BAYERN-SÜD)
(May be administratively combined with 13 - Gruppe Main-Donau)

TERRITORY (Parteigau):	München-Oberbayern, Schwaben, Tirol-Vorarlberg
HQ:	MÜNCHEN 2, Theresienstr. 84
COMMAND:	OGF. Carl BRAUN, Oberst der Luftwaffe CoS Staf Karl von BLOMBERG
COMPONENT STANDARTEN:	94 95 96 97 98
SCHOOLS CONTROLLED BY GRUPPE:	Flugzeugführerschule Sonthofen Segelflugschule Schwangau

15 - SCHWABEN

TERRITORY (Parteigau):	Württemberg-Hohenzollern
HQ:	STUTTGART, Neckarstr. 195
COMMAND:	GF. ERBACHER, Führer OF. KELLNER, Stabs- u. Kriegsführer
COMPONENT STANDARTEN:	101 102 103 104 107
SCHOOLS CONTROLLED BY GRUPPE:	Segelflugbauschule Esslingen Segelflugschule Hornberg " Weilheim an der Teck " Dettingen " Wachtersberg

Note:- In 1940, according to the document given as Annexe E, this unit was known as NSFK Brig 125 Weichselland; the 1943 Organisationsbuch der NSDAP shows it as Brig 21 'WEICHSELLAND'.

16 - SÜDWEST

TERRITORY (Parteigau):	Baden, Westmark, Elsass
HQ:	STRASSBURG, Schwarzwaldstr. 26
COMMAND:	GF. Ferdinand v. HIDDESEN, Führer OF. Arno GLEISNER, Stabsführer
COMPONENT STANDARTEN:	79 80 81 82 83 84
SCHOOLS CONTROLLED BY GRUPPE:	Flugzeugführerschule Freiburg " Mannheim " Karlsruhe

17 - DONAU - ALPENLAND

TERRITORY (Parteigau):	Kärnten, Niederdonau, Oberdonau, Steiermark, Wien
HQ:	WIEN III, Metternichg. 6
COMMAND:	GF. Alfred KRÜGER OF. SELLING, Stabsführer
COMPONENT STANDARTEN:	111 112 113 114 115 116 201
SCHOOLS CONTROLLED BY GRUPPE:	Flugzeugführerschule Aigen Flugmodellbauschule Gmunden Segelflugschule Spitzenberg " Zell am See Segelfluglager Herzogenburg (N.D.)

18 - WEICHSELLAND (formerly NSFK-Brigade 125)

(See Gruppe 5 - Wartheland)

EINHEIT GENERALGOUVERNMENT:

This unit is shown in the 1943 Organisationsbuch as being independent of any Gruppe and apparently ranking level with the Gruppen. For details of component units see Annexe E.
According to PW Report of Feb 45, the Einheit GG has, for the duration, been administered combined with Gruppe 5 (q.v.)

PART TWO

NSFK STANDARTEN

NO:	HQ LOCATION:	GRUPPE:	COMMANDER:	COMPONENT UNITS:
1	Königsberg, Hintertragg. 18	1		1/1 Königsberg 2/1 " 3/1 " 4/1 " 7/1 Insterburg 8/1 Tilsit 9/1 Pr. Eylau 14/1 Memel

2	Allenstein "HELMUT KIRSCHKE" Schanzenstr.	1		2/2 Bartenstein
				   Heilsburg
				3/2 Pr. Holland
				4/2 Ortelsburg
				5/2 Rastenburg
				   Sensburg
				6/2 Ortelsburg
				7/2 Lötzen
				8/2 Soldau
				9/2 Lyck
				
				11/2 Plock

3	Elbing	1	SF. SCHWARZGRUBER	1/3 Elbing
				   Gumbinnen
				
				4/3 Tilsit-Waldhof
				   Pr. Holland
				5/3 Insterburg
				6/3 Marienburg
				   Goldap

4	Danzig	5		1/4 Danzig 2/4 " 3/4 "

NO:	HQ LOCATION:	GRUPPE:	COMMANDER:	COMPONENT UNITS:
5				
6				
7				
8	Schneidemühl	2/4		1/8 Lauerberg
				2/8 Neustettin
				5/8 Schneidemühl
				7/8 Köslin
				10/8 Kolberg
				11/8 Belgard
9				

NO:	HQ LOCATION:	GRUPPE:	COMMANDER:	COMPONENT UNITS:	
10	Stettin	2/4		1/10	Naugard
				2/10	Stargard
				3/10	Pyritz
				4/10	Cammin
				5/10	Stettin
				6/10	"
				7/10	"
				8/10	
				9/10	Greifenhagen
				10/10	Swinemünde
11	Stralsund Heiligegeiststr. 76	2/4	OSBF HOTH	2/11	Stralsund
				3/11	Greifswald
				4/11	Ribnitz
				5/11	Anklam
				9/11	Waren
12	Schwerin Körnerstr. 22	2/4	SBF BAUER	1/12	Güstrow
				2/12	Rostock
				3/12	Marienehe
				4/12	Warnemünde
				5/12	Domsühl
				6/12	Festung Dömitz
				9/12	Schwerin
13					
14		?2/4		1/14	Soldin

NO:	HQ LOCATION:	GRUPPE:	COMMANDER:	COMPONENT UNITS:	
15	Hamburg	3/9	SF REINHOLD	1/15	Hamburg
				2/15	Fuhlsbüttel
				3/15	Wandsbeck
				4/15	Hamburg
				5/15	Bergedorf
				6/15	Altona
				7/15	Harburg
				8/15	"
				9/15	"
				10/15	Lokstedt
				11/15	Altona
				12/15	Hamburg
				14/15	Cuxhaven
16	Neumünster	3/9	OSBF MILBERT	1/16	Kiel
				5/16	Eutin
				6/16	Lübeck
				7/16	Lauenburg
				9/16	Ütersen
				11/16	Heide
				12/16	Preetz
				14/16	Kiel
17	Oldenburg	3/9		1/17	Oldenburg
				2/17	Bremen
				3/17	"
				4/17	"
				5/17	Wilhelmshafen
				6/17	Norden
				7/17	Emden
				8/17	Vechta
				10/17	Zuakenbrück
				11/17	Osnabrück
				13/17	Delmenhorst
18	Lüneburg	3/9		1/18	Lüneburg
				3/18	Walsrode
				5/18	Walsrode
				6/18	Celle
				8/18	Buchholz

NO:	HQ LOCATION:	GRUPPE:	COMMANDER:	COMPONENT UNITS:	
19					
20					
21					
22	Frankfurt/O	2/4		1/22	Frankfurt/O
				2/22	Fürstenwalde
				3/22	Königsberg
				4/22	Küstrin
				5/22	Landsberg

NO:	HQ LOCATION:	GRUPPE:	COMMANDER:	COMPONENT UNITS:	
23	Cottbus	2/4		1/23	Finsterwalde
				2/23	Senftenberg
				4/23	Cottbus
				5/23	Spremberg
				6/23	Forst
				8/23	Sorau
				9/23	Gruben
24	Neuruppin Steinstr. 20	2/4		1/24	Perleberg
				3/24	Neuruppin
				6/24	Angermünde
				8/24	Eberswalde Bad Freienwalde
25	Potsdam	2/4		4/25	Brandenburg
				7/25	Zossen
				11/25	Jüterbog
26	Berlin	2/4	?OSBF SIEVERT possible Cdr. Sta 27.		

NO:	HQ LOCATION:	GRUPPE:	COMMANDER:	COMPONENT UNITS:	
27	Berlin	2/4	see Sta 26		
28					
29	Oppeln Sedanstr. 17	6	SF ULLRICH WÖLL	1/29 2/29 3/29 4/29 5/29 8/29 9/29 11/29	Gleiwitz Loben (Lublinitz) Gr. Strehlen Leobschütz Ratibor Kreuzburg Gr. Strelitz Neisse
30	Breslau Tauenzienstr. 29	6		1-6/30 8/30 9/30 10/30 12/30	Breslau Strehlen Brieg Oels Breslau/Lissa
31	Beuthen	6		1/31 2/31 3/31 4/31 5/31 6/31 7/31 8/31 9/31	Hirschberg Landeshut Waldenburg Braunau Glatz Hohenelbe Frankenstein Reichenbach Freiburg

NO:	HQ LOCATION:	GRUPPE:	COMMANDER:	COMPONENT UNITS:	
32	Görlitz Biesnitzerstr.33	6	OSBF SCHÄFER	1/32	Liegnitz
				3/32	Grünberg
				4/32	Sprottau
				5/32	Weisswasser
				7/32	Görlitz
				8/32	Lauban
				9/32	Bunzlau
				10/32	Haynau
33	Jägerndorf (Ostsudetenland) Adolf-Hitler Pl.22	6		1/33	Jägerndorf
				2/33	Troppau
				3/33	Neutitschein
				4/33	Bautsch
				5/33	Sternberg
				6/33	Freudenthal
				7/33	Freiwaldau
				8/33	Mähr. Schönberg
				9/33	Hohenstadt
				10/33	Zwittau
34	Kattowitz Grundmannstrasse 33	6	SF SASSMANNS-HAUSEN	1/34	Tarnowitz
				4/34	Chergow
				6/34	Kattowitz
				7/34	Myslowitz
				8/34	Scharley Nikolai ?
				9/34	Rybnik
				10/34	Mechtel
				12/34	Radzionkau-Buchatz/Scharley
				13/34	Kattowitz
35	Bielitz Beskidenstr.3	6	SF DESCHER	1/35	Ratibor
				3/35	Rybnik
				4/35	Nikolai
				5/35	Freistadt
				7/35	Bielitz

NO:	HQ LOCATION:	GRUPPE:	COMMANDER:	COMPONENT UNITS:	
36	Halle/S Hermann-Goering Strasse 1	7	OSBF FRIEDRICH HINZ	1/36	Halle/S
				3/36	Eilenburg
				5/36	Eisleben
				6/36	Sangershausen
				7/36	Naumburg
				8/36	Zeitz
				9/36	Merseburg
				10/36	Torgau
				11/36	Wittenberg
				13/36	Halle/S
37	Chemnitz	7	SF BERTRAM	1/37	Chemnitz
				2/37	"
				3/37	"
				4/37	"
				5/37	"
				6/37	Annaberg-Buchholz
				7/37	Aue
				8/37	Hartenstein
				9/37	Zwickau
				10/37	Laucha
				11/37	Falkenstein
				12/37	Plauen
38	Dresden	7	OSBF FISCHER	1/38	Dresden
				2/38	Dresden
				3/38	Dresden
				4/38	Freiburg ?
				5/38	Bad Schandau
				6/38	Zittau
				8/38	Meissen
				10/38	Meissen
				11/38	Grossenhain
39	Leipzig	7	OSBF ADOLF POPP	1/39	Leipzig
				2/39	Leipzig
				5/39	Taucha
				7/39	Döbeln

NO:	HQ LOCATION:	GRUPPE:	COMMANDER:	COMPONENT UNITS:	
40	Teplitz-Schönau Nordstr. 5	7	SF FERDINAND DITTRICH	1/40	Gablonz
				2/40	Reichenberg
				3/40	Warnsdorf
				4/40	Böhm. Leipa
				6/40	Aussig
				7/40	Kosten
				8/40	Dux
				10/40	Komotau
				12/40	Karlsbad
				13/40	Falkenau
				17/40	Leitmeritz
					Teschen ?
				18/40	Prag
41					
42					
43	Weimar Ludendorfstr. 28	8		1/43	Altenburg
				2/43	Gera
				3/43	Greiz
				4/43	Schleiz
				5/43	Saalfeld
				6/43	Rudolstadt
				7/43	Ilmenau
				8/43	Arnstadt
				9/43	Erfurt
				10/43	Weimar

NO:	HQ LOCATION:	GRUPPE:	COMMANDER:	COMPONENT UNITS:	
44	Gotha	3		1/44	Sonneburg
				2/44	Hildburghausen
				3/44	Zella-Mehlis
				4/44	Meiningen
				5/44	Vacha
				6/44	Schmalkalden
				7/44	Waltershausen
				8/44	Eisenach
				9/44	Gotha
				10/44	Langensalza
				12/44	Sondershausen
45	Kassel Germaniastr. 1½	8		1/45	Eschwege
				3/45	Fulda
				4/45	Homberg
				5/45	Marburg/L
				6/45	Bad Wildungen
				7/45	Hofgeismar
46					
47					

NO:	HQ LOCATION:	GRUPPE:	COMMANDER:	COMPONENT UNITS:
48		? 8		
				11/48 Heiligenstadt
49				
50	Hannover	3/9		1/50 Hannover
				2/50 "
				3/50 "
				4/50 Peine
				Hildesheim
				5/50 Braunschweig
				6/50 "
				8/50 Helmstedt
				12/50 Göttingen
				13/50 Northeim
				15/50 Holzminden
				17/50 Hildesheim ?
51				

NO:	HQ LOCATION:	GRUPPE:	COMMANDER:	COMPONENT UNITS:	
52	Magdeburg Gr. Kloster- strasse 16	3/9		1/52 2/52	Magdeburg "
				4/52 5/52 III/5/52 6/52 7/52	Haldensleben Gardelegen Badersleben Salzwedel Stendal
				18/52	Oschersleben
53	Dessau Kaiserstr. 4	3/9	SF FRIEDEL	?/53	Dessau
				4/53	Köthen
				7/53 8/53	Stassfurt Aschersleben
				10/53 11/53	Halberstadt Wernigerode
54					
55					

A 20

NO:	HQ LOCATION:	GRUPPE:	COMMANDER:	COMPONENT UNITS:	
56					
57	Dortmund Reinholdis- strasse 19	10	OSBF LEHN	1/57 2/57 3/57 4/57 5/57 6/57 7/57 8/57	Dortmund " Bochum Wanne-Eickel Hattingen Hagen Schwerte Gevelsberg
58	Arnsberg Bahnhofstr. 65-66	10		1/58 3/58 4/58 5/58 6/58 7/58 8/58 9/58	Iserlohn Ludenscheid Lippstadt Altendorf Meschede Siegen Hamm Neheim
59	Münster i. Westf. Hermannstr. 63	10		2/59 3/59 4/59 6/59 7/59 8/59 9/59	Münster Telgte Greven Rheine Recklinghausen Gladbeck Bielefeld Gelsenkirchen "

NO:	HQ LOCATION:	GRUPPE:	COMMANDER:	COMPONENT UNITS:	
60	Detmold Elizabethstrasse 38	?9 or 10		1/60	Detmold
				2/60	Paderborn
				4/60	Bückeburg
				5/60	Minden
				8/60	Gütersloh
				9/60	Lübbecke
				11/60	Bünde
61	Hannover Hohenzollernstrasse 42	?9 or 10		4/61	Wanne
				7/61	Gladbeck

NO:	HQ LOCATION:	GRUPPE:	COMMANDER:	COMPONENT UNITS:	
65	Köln Hohenstaufen- ring 45	11/12		1/65 2/65 3/65 4/65 5/65 7/65 8/65 9/65 10/65	Köln " Bonn Siegburg Wipperfürth Aachen Eschweiler Jülich Düren Eupen
66	Düsseldorf	11/12		1/66 2/66 4/66 5/66 6/66 7/66 8/66 9/66 10/66 11/66 12/66	Düsseldorf " Krefeld M. Gladbach Kempen Neuss Langenberg Wuppertal " Solingen Remscheid
67	Mülheim	11/12		1/67 2/67 3/67 4/67 5/67 6/67 7/67	Essen Mülheim/Ruhr Duisberg Oberhausen Eppinghofen Moers Emmerich
68					

NO:	HK LOCATION:	GRUPPE:	COMMANDER:	COMPONENT UNITS:
69				
70	Gelsenkirchen	10		
71				

72	Koblenz Goeben-platz 11	11 12		1/72 Koblenz
				2/72 Bad Kreuznach
				3/72 Trier
				4/72 Traben-Trarbach
				5/72 Neuwied
				6/72 Linz (Rhein)
				  Wiesen (Siegkreis)
				  or Wissen
				    (Kr. Altenkirchen)

NO:	HQ LOCATION:	GRUPPE:	COMMANDER:	COMPONENT UNITS:	
73					
74					
75	Frankfurt/M Fellnestr. 6	11/12	HSF KITTNER	1/75	Frankfurt/M
				2/75	"
				3/75	Bad Homburg
				5/75	Gelnhausen
				7/75	Wetzlar
				8/75	Diez
				10/75	Frankfurt/M
				11/75	Wiesbaden
				12/75	Frankfurt/M
76					
77	Darmstadt	11/12		2/77	Offenbach/M
				3/77	Dieburg
				5/77	Stockstadt/M

A 25

NO:	HQ LOCATION:	GRUPPE:	COMMANDER:	COMPONENT UNITS:	
78	Luxemburg Prinzenring 43	11/12		2/78 3/78	Offenbach/M Esch-Alzig
				6/78	Wittlich
79	Mannheim	16			
80	Karlsruhe	16		2/80	Mosbach
				?4/80 5/80 6/80	Mannheim Bruchsal Karlsruhe
				8/80	Pforzheim
81	Neustadt/Weinstr.	16		1/81 2/81 3/81 4/81	Germersheim Ludwigshafen Kaiserslautern Pirmasens
				6/81	St. Ingbert/Saar
				8/81 9/81 10/81	Landsweiler Sulzbach Saarbrücken
				12/81	Saarlautern

NO:	HQ LOCATION:	GRUPPE:	COMMANDER:	COMPONENT UNITS:	
82	Mülhausen	16	SBF MEYER	1/82	Rastatt ?
				2/82	Kolmar
				3/82	Haslach ?
				4/82	Freiburg
				8/82	Singen
				9/82	Konstanz
				10/82	Tann
				11/82	Altkirch
				12/82	Mülhausen
83	Strassburg	16		1/83	Rastatt ?
				3/83	Haslach ?
				5/83	Zabern
				6/83	Hagenau
				7/83	Strassburg
				8/83	"
				9/83	Molsheim
				11/83	Schlettstadt
84	Metz Rosenstr. 18	16	SS SF KEMPEN	2/84	Metz - Süd
				4/84	Diedenhofen
				7/84	Saargemund
				8/84	Saarburg

NO:	HQ LOCATION:	GRUPPE:	COMMANDER:	COMPONENT UNITS:	
87	Nürnberg	13	HSF ROITHMEIER	1/87	Nürnberg
				3/87	Fürth
				4/87	Erlangen
				5/87	Laufen
				6/87	Schwabach
				7/87	Weissenburg
				8/87	Ansbach
				9/87	Neustadt/Aisch
				10/87	Fürth
88	Würzburg Schönleinstrasse 9	13		1/88	Würzburg
				2/88	Kitzingen a/M
				3/88	Würzburg
				7/88	Würzburg
89	Kulmbach	13	HSF HUPFAUF	1/89	Bayreuth
				4/89	Bamberg
				5/89	Coburg
				8/89	Selb
				9/89	Marktredwitz
				11/89	Weiden
90	Regensburg	13	OSF GRAF	1/90	Regensburg
				2/90	Straubing
				3/90	Schwandorf
				4/90	Passau
				5/90	Landshut
				7/90	Deggendorf
91	Eger	13		1/91	Eger
				2/91	Asch
				5/91	Franzensbad

A 28

NO:	HQ LOCATION:	GRUPPE:	COMMANDER:	COMPONENT UNITS:	
92					
93					
94	München	13/14 ?			
				4/94	München
				9/94	Starnberg
				12/94	Schrobenhausen
				14/94	Augsburg
95	Augsburg "ERWIN AICHELE" Klingerberg 7	13/14 ?	OSF OVERBORG (also Cdr.Sta 96)	1/95	Augsburg
				10/95	Gablingen
96		13/14	(see Sta 95)		
				4/96	Kaufbeuren
				6/96	Blaichach/Allgäu

NO:	HQ LOCATION:	GRUPPE:	COMMANDER:	COMPONENT UNITS:	
97	München	13/14 ?		1/97	Wolfratshausen
				2/97	Holzkirchen
				4/97	Prien
					Rosenheim
				5/97	Traunstein
				9/97	Garmisch-Partenkirchen
98	Innsbruck Müllerstr.13	13/14 ?	OSF ROLAND HOCHRAINER	1/98	Innsbruck
				4/98	Lustenau
				5/98	Bregenz
				6/98	Blaibach
				?	Kufstein
99					
100					

NO:	HQ LOCATION:	GRUPPE:	COMMANDER:	COMPONENT UNITS:	
101	Stuttgart Rosenbergstrasse 1	15			
				4/101	Wildbad
				6/101	Böblingen
				7/101	Tübingen
				8/101	Esslingen
102	Heilbronn Bicherestr.52	15			
				2/102	Schwäb. Hall
				3/102	Bad Mergentheim
				5/102	Bietigheim
				6/102	Schwäb. Gmünd
				9/102	Esslingen
103	Friedrichshafen Allmandstr.47	15	OSBF SCHUMACHER	1/103	Friedrichshafen
				5/103	Biberach
				6/103	Ulm
				7/103	Kirchheim
				8/103	Reutlingen
				10/103	Balingen
104	Schwenningen	15			
				9/104	Schwenningen
105					

NO:	HQ LOCATION:	GRUPPE:	COMMANDER:	COMPONENT UNITS:
106				
107	Heilbronn	15		1/107 Heilbronn
				5/107 Offenburg
				12/107 Haslach
108				
109				
110				

NO:	HQ LOCATION:	GRUPPE:	COMMANDER:	COMPONENT UNITS:	
111	Linz/D Kroatengasse 21	17		1/111	Linz/D
				2/111	"
				III/2/111	Wels
				5/111	Gmunden
				7/111	Steyr
				8/111	Freistadt
				10/111	Braunau
				12/111	Krumau
				15/111	Gratzen
112	Wien IX/71 Währingerstrasse 17	17	SF MÜLLER-KLINGSPOR	1/112	Wien
				2/112	"
				3/112	
				4/112	
				6/112	Wien Mödling Wiener-Neustadt
				10/112	Wien
				12/112	Wien
113	Klagenfurt	17	HSF RUDL	1/113	Klagenfurt
				3/113	St. Veit
				4/113	Lienz
				6/113	Villach
				8/113	Krainburg
114	Znaim Salispl.17	17		7/114	Brünn

NO:	HQ LOCATION:	GRUPPE:	COMMANDER:	COMPONENT UNITS:	
115	Graz Krefelderstrasse 31/I	17		1/115 2/115 3/115 4/115 5/115 6/115	Graz " Leibnitz Leoben Steinach Mürzzuschlag
116	Wien ("Niederdonau") IV/50 Schwindg.18	17	OSBF SCHULZEHULBE	1/116 2/116 4/116 6/116 7/116 9/116 11/116 12/116	Krems Melk Wilhelmsburg Baden bei Wien Hainburg Stockerau Nikolsburg Znaim
117					
118					
119	Litzmannstadt	5	SF WILHELM LEHSTER	4/119 5/119	Pabianice Ostrowo

NO:	IN LOCATION:	GRUPPE:	COMMANDER:	COMPONENT UNITS:
120	Hohensalza	5		1/120 Hohensalza
				2/120 Gnesen
				5/120 Leslau
121	Posen	5	Ustuf NIEMANN	
				9/121 Lissa
122				
123				
124				

A 35

NO:	HQ LOCATION:	GRUPPE:	COMMANDER:	COMPONENT UNITS:	
125	Danzig "Brig. Weichsel-land"	5	GF BRAND (also Cdr. Sta.126)		
				9/125	Dirschau
126	Bromberg	5	(see Sta 125)	2/126 3/126	Thorn Zempelburg
127					
128					
129	Naugard	2			

NO:	HQ LOCATION:	GRUPPE:	COMMANDER:	COMPONENT UNITS:
201	Salzburg	17		1/201 Salzburg
457	Herne ? Adolf-Hitler Platz 4			

CONFIDENTIAL

SUPREME HEADQUARTERS ALLIED EXPEDITIONARY FORCE
EVALUATION AND DISSEMINATION SECTION
G-2 (COUNTER INTELLIGENCE SUB-DIVISION)

BASIC HANDBOOK OF THE NSFK

ANNEXE B

Diagrams and Plates

E.D.S./G/2
Compiled by MIRS (LONDON Branch)
From Material Available at
WASHINGTON and LONDON

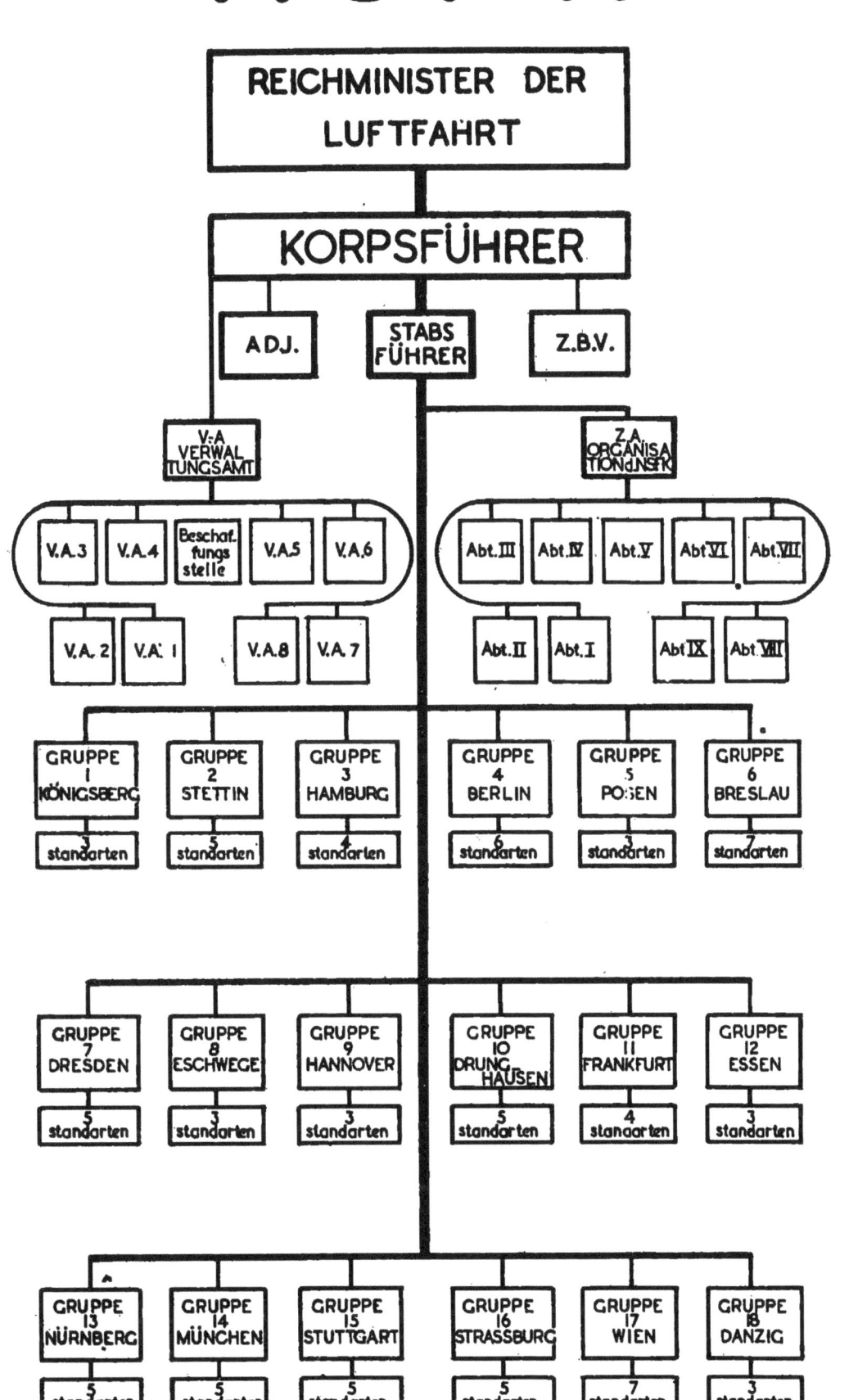

NSFK
Table of Organisation
Based on the 1943 ORGANISATIONSBUCH der NSDAP

DIAGRAM — B
ANNEXE

Reichsminister der Luftfahrt

KORPSFÜHRUNG

- **KORPSFÜHRER**
  - Adj.
  - Z.B.V.
  - Inspekteur
  - Ständiger bevollmächtigter Vertreter des Korpsführers und Chef des Stabes
    - Ausbildungsamt
    - Personalamt
    - Führungsamt
    - Sanitätsamt
    - Verwaltungsamt

for further notes on Korpsführung see Text Para. ()

Gruppen (Groups)

1. OSTPREUSSEN (OSTLAND)
2. OSTSEE
3. NORDWEST
4. BERLIN-BRANDENBURG
5. WARTHELAND
6. SCHLESIEN
7. ELBE-SAALE
8. MITTE
9. WESER-ELBE
10. WESTFALEN
11. MOSELLAND-HESSEN-WESTMARK
12. NIEDERRHEIN
13. MAIN-DONAU
14. HOCHLAND
15. WÜRTTEMBERG (SCHWABEN)
16. SÜDWEST
17. DONAU-ALPENLAND
18. WEICHSELLAND

See Annexe A. (Later information)

18 GROUPS & Einsatz General.Gouvernement

(EACH GROUP from 3-7 REGTS)

GROUP — Regt., Regt., Regt., Regt.

(EACH REGT. 10-12 COYS.)

REGT. — COY, COY, COY, COY, COY, COY, COY, COY

One Exceptional REGT. is Believed to contain 18 COYS

NSFK
Table of Organisation
Based on the '1943 ORGANISATIONSBUCH der NSDAP.'

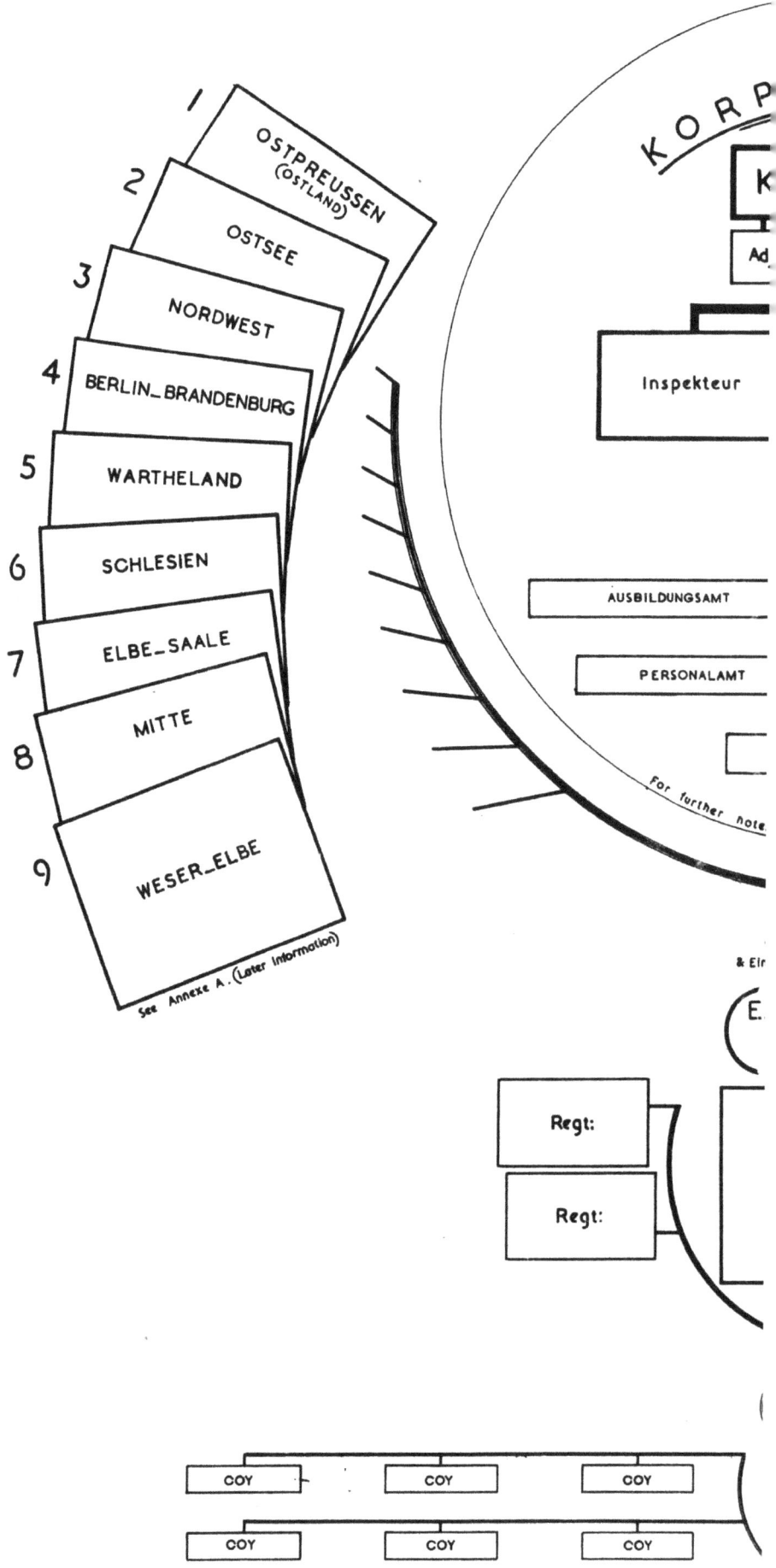

1. OSTPREUSSEN (OSTLAND)
2. OSTSEE
3. NORDWEST
4. BERLIN-BRANDENBURG
5. WARTHELAND
6. SCHLESIEN
7. ELBE-SAALE
8. MITTE
9. WESER-ELBE

See Annexe A. (Later Information)

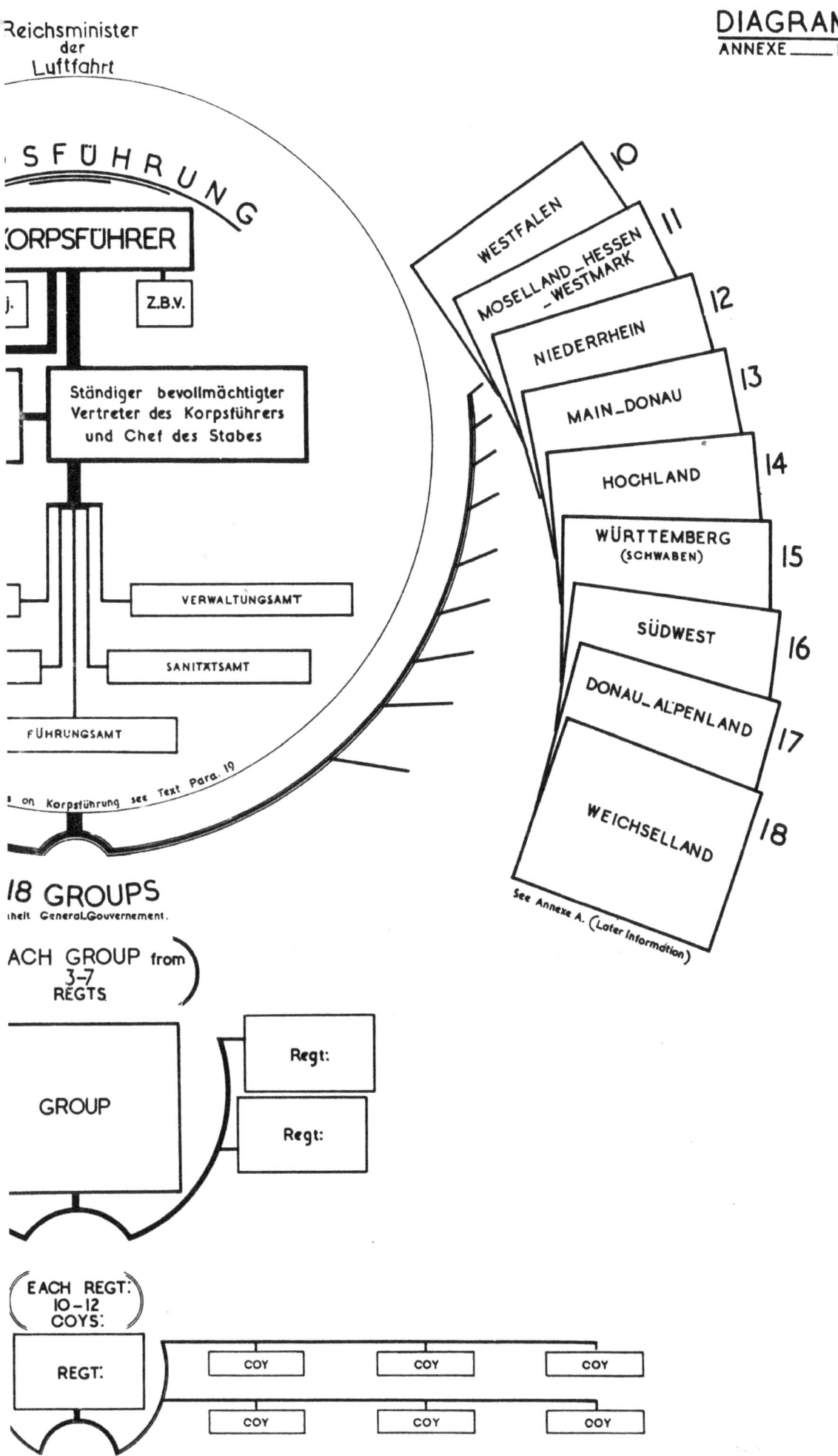

Uniformen des NS.-Fliegerkorps

NSFK.-Rottenführer
im großen Dienstanzug

NSFK.-Obersturmbannführer
im kleinen Dienstanzug

NSFK.-Sturmführer
in der Korpsführung
im Ausgehanzug

NSFK.-Scharführer
im Abendanzug
Sturm 4 der Standarte 39

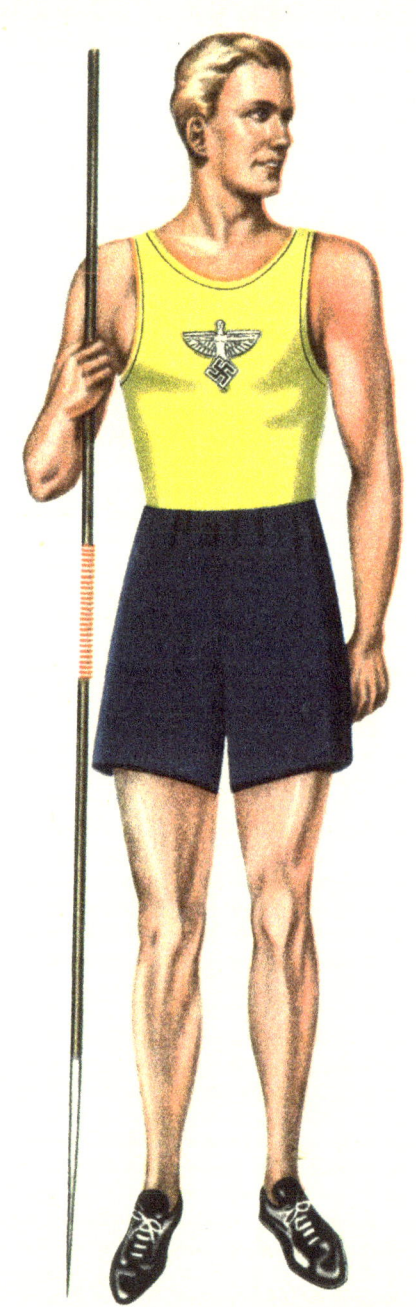

NSFK.-Scharführer
im Dienstmantel

NSFK.-Mann
im Sportanzug

Dienstgradabzeichen des NSFK.

NSFK.-Mann   Sturmmann   Rottenführer   Scharführer

Oberscharführer   Truppführer   Obertruppführer   Sturmführer

Obersturmführer   Sturmhauptführer   Sturmbannführer   Obersturmbannführer

Standartenführer   Oberführer   Brigadeführer

Gruppenführer   Obergruppenführer   Korpsführer

CONFIDENTIAL

SUPREME HEADQUARTERS ALLIED EXPEDITIONARY FORCE
EVALUATION AND DISSEMINATION SECTION
G-2 (COUNTER INTELLIGENCE SUB-DIVISION)

BASIC HANDBOOK OF THE NSFK

ANNEXE C

Gazetteer

E.D.S./G/2
Compiled by MIRS (LONDON Branch)
From Material Available at
WASHINGTON and LONDON

ANNEXE C

NSFK GAZETTEER

(List of identified locations of NSFK Units, H.Q. and Establishments)

LOCATION	UNIT(S)	ESTABLISHMENTS
Aachen	7/65	
Aigen		Flugzeugführerschule (Pilot School)
Allenstein	Stand. 2.	Flugzeugführerschule (Pilot School)
Altenburg	1/43	
Altendorf	5/58	
Altkirch	11/82	
Altona	6/15, 11/15	Reichsschule für Motorflugsport (National School for Motor Aviation Sports)
Angermünde	6/24	
Anklam	5/11	
Annaberg-Buchholz	6/37	
Ansbach	8/87	
Arnsberg	Stand. 58	
Arnstadt	8/43	
Asch	2/91	
Aschersleben	8/53	
Aue	7/37	
Augsburg	Stand. 95, 14/94, 1/95	
Aussig	6/40	
Bad Freienwalde	8/24	
Bad Homburg	3/75	
Bad Kreuznach	2/72	
Bad Mergentheim	3/102	
Bad Schandau	5/38	
Bad Wildungen	6/45	
Baden bei Wien	6/116	
Badersleben	III/5/52	
Balingen	10/103	
Ballenstedt		Segelflugschule (Glider School)
Bamberg	4/89	
Bartenstein	2/2	
Bautsch	4/33	
Bayreuth	1/89	
Belgard	11/8	
Bergedorf	5/15	
Berlin	Stand. 26, 27	Gr. 4-Berlin-Brandenburg
Beuthen	Stand. 31	
Biberach	5/103	

LOCATION	UNIT(S)	ESTABLISHMENTS
Bielefeld	7/59	Flugzeugführerschule (Pilot School)
Bielitz	Stand. 35, 7/35	
Bietigheim	5/102	
Blaibach	6/98	
Blaichach/Allgäu	6/96	
Bochum	3/57	
Böblingen	6/101	
Böhm. Leipa	4/40	
Bonn	3/65	
Borkenberge		Segelflugschule (Glider School)
Brandenburg	4/25	
Braunau	4/31, 10/111	
Braunschweig	5/50, 6/50	Flugzeugführerschule (Pilot School)
Bregenz	5/98	
Bremen	2-4/17	
Breslau	Stand. 30, 1-6/30	Gr. 6-Schlesien
Breslau-Gandau		Flugzeugführerschule (Pilot School)
Breslau/Lissa	12/30	
Brieg	9/30	
Bromberg	Stand. 126	
Bruchsal	5/80	
Brünn	7/114	
Buchholz	8/18	
Bückeburg	4/60	
Bünde	11/60	
Bunzlau	9/32	Flugmodellbauschule
Cammin	4/10	
Celle	6/18	
Chemnitz	Stand. 37, 1-5/37	Reichsschule für Motorflugsport (National School for Motor Aviation sports) and Flugzeugführerschule
Chergow	4/34	
Coburg	5/89	
Cottbus	Stand. 23, 4/23	
Cuxhaven	14/15	
Danzig	Stand. 4, 125 1-3/4	Gr.-18-Wiechselland (formerly NSFK Brigade 125)
Darmstadt	Stand. 77	
Deggendorf	7/90	
Delmenhorst	13/17	
Dessau	Stand. 53	
Detmold	Stand. 60, 1/60	

LOCATION	UNIT(S)	ESTABLISHMENTS
Dettingen		Segelflugschule (Glider School)
Deuthen b. Allenstein		Werkstattleiterschule (Workshop Instructors' School)
Dieburg	3/77	
Diedenhofen	4/84	
Diez	3/75	
Dinkelsbühl		Werkstattleiterschule (Workshop Instructors' School)
Dirschau	9/125	
Döbeln	7/39	
Dörnberg		Segelflugschule (Glider School)
Donsühl	5/12	
Dortmund	Stand. 57, 1-2/57	
Dresden	Stand. 38, 1-3/38	Gr. 7 -Elbe-Saale
Dresden-Heller		Flugzeugführerschule (Pilot School)
Duisberg	3/67	
Düren	9/65	
Düsseldorf	Stand. 66, 1-2/66	
Dux	8/40	
Eberswalde	8/24	
Eger	Stand. 91 1/91	
Eilenburg	3/36	
Eisenach	8/44	
Eisleben	5/36	
Elbing	Stand. 3, 1/3	
Emden	7/17	
Emmerich	7/67	
Eppinghofen	5/67	
Erfurt	9/43	Flugzeugführerschule (Pilot School)
Erlangen	4/87	
Esch-Alzig	3/78	
Eschwege	1/45	Gr. 8-Mitte
Eschweiler	7/65	
Essen	1/67	Gr. 12-Niederrhein
Esslingen	8/101, 9/102	Segelflugbauschule (Glider Construction School)
Eupen	10/65	
Eutin	5/16	

LOCATION	UNIT(S)	ESTABLISHMENTS
Falkenau	13/40	
Falkenstein	11/37	
Festung Dömitz	6/12	
Finsterwalde	1/23	
Fischbeck		Segelflugschule
Forst	6/23	
Frankenstein	7/31	
Frankfurt/M	Stand. 75, 1-2/75, 10/75, 12/75	Gr. 11-Moselland-Hessen-Westmark
Frankfurt/O	Stand. 22, 1/22	
Frankfurt-Rebstock		Flugzeugführerschule (Pilot School)
Franzensbad	5/91	
Freiburg	9/31, 4/38, 4/82	Flugzeugführerschule (Pilot School)
Freistadt	5/35, 8/111	
Freiwaldau	7/33	
Freudenthal	6/33	
Friedrichshafen	Stand. 103, 1/103	
Furstenberg/O		Segelflugbauschule (Glider Construction School)
Fürstenwalde	2/22	
Fürth	3/87, 10/87	
Fulda	3/45	
Gablingen	10/95	
Gablonz	1/40	
Gandau		Reichsflugschule (National School of Aviation)
Gardelegen	5/52	
Garmisch-Partenkirchen	9/97	
Gelnhausen	5/75	
Gelsenkirchen	Stand. 70, -9/59	
Gelsenkirchen-Buer		Flugzeugführerschule (Pilot School)
Gemersheim	1/81	
Gevelsberg	8/57	
Gladbeck	7/59, 7/61	
Glatz	5/31	
Gleiwitz	1/29	
Gmunden	5/111	Flugmodellbauschule
Gnesen	2/120	
Görlitz	Stand. 32, 7/32	
Göttingen	12/50	
Goldap	6/3	
Gitter		Segelflugschule
Gera	2/43	
Greiz	3/43	

LOCATION	UNIT(S)	ESTABLISHMENTS
Gotha	Stand. 44, 9/44	
Gratzen	15/111	
Graz	Stand. 115, 1-2/115	Motorsportschule
Greifenhasen	9/10	
Greifswald	3/11	
Greiz	3/43	
Greven	3/59	
Gr. Strehlen	3/29	
Gr. Strelitz	9/29	
Grossenhain	11/38	
Grossbrückerswalde		Segelflugschule
Grünberg	3/32	
Guben	9/23	
Güstrow	1/12	
Gütersloh	8/60	
Gumbinnen	1/3	
Hagen	6/57	
Hagenau	6/83	
Hainburg	7/116	
Halberstadt	10/53	
Haldensleben	4/52	
Halle/S	Stand. 36 1/36, 13/36	
Haltingen	5/57	
Hamburg	Stand.15, 1/15, 4/15, 12/15	Gr. 3-Nordwest
Hamburg-Fuhlsbüttel	2/15	Flugzeugführerschule
Hamburg-Wandsbeck		Segelflugbauschule
Hamm	8/58	
Hannover	Stand. 50, 61 1-3/50	Gr. 9-Weser-Elbe Werkstattleiterschule
Harburg	7-9/15	
Harsberg		Segelflugschule
Hartenstein	8/37	
Haslach	12/107, 3/82, 3/83	
Hattingen	5/57	
Haynau	10/32	
Heide	11/16	
Heilbronn	Stand. 102, 107, 1/107	
Heiligenstadt	11/48	
Heilsburg	2/2	
Helmstedt	8/50	
Herne ?		
Herzogenburg ND		Segelfluglager
Hesselberg		Segelflugschule
Hildburghausen	2/44	
Hildesheim	4/50, 17/50	
Hirschberg	1/31	Reichsschule für Segelflugsport
Hirzenhain (Dillkr.)		Segelfluglager

LOCATION	UNIT(S)	ESTABLISHMENTS
Hofgeismar	7/45	
Hohenelbe	6/31	
Hohensalza	Stand. 120, 1/120	
Hohenstadt	9/33	
Holzkirchen	2/97	
Holzminden	15/50	
Homberg	4/45	
Hornberg		Reichsschulen für Segelflugsport
Hummerich		Segelflugschule
Ilmenau	7/43	
Innsbruck	Stand. 98 1/98	
Insterburg	7/1, 5/3	
Iserlohn	1/58	
Ith		Segelflugschule
Jägerndorf	Stand. 33, 1/33	
Jülich	8/65	
Jüterbog	11/25	
Kaiserslautern	3/81	
Kamenz		Segelflugbauschule
Karlsbad	12/40	
Karlsruhe	Stand. 80, 6/80	Reichsschule für Motorflugsport and Flugzeugführerschule
Kassel	Stand. 45,	
Kattowitz	Stand. 34, 6/34, 13/34	
Kaufbeuren	4/96	
Kempen	6/66	
Kiel	1/16, 14/16	
Kirchheim	7/103	
Kirschberg	1/31	
Kitzingen/M	2/88	
Klagenfurt	Stand. 113, 1/113	
Koblenz	Stand. 72, 1/72	
Köln	Stand. 65, 1-2/65	Reichsschule für Motorflugsport Gr. 1-OSTLAND Flugzeugführerschule
Königsberg	3/22	
Königsberg/PR	Stand. 1, 1-3/1, 4/1	
Köslin	7/8	
Köthen	4/53	
Kolberg	10/8	
Kolmar	2/82	
Komotau	10/40	
Konstanz	9/82	
Kosten	7/40	
Krainburg	8/113	

LOCATION	UNIT(S)	ESTABLISHMENTS
Krefeld	4/66	
Krems	1/116	
Kreuzburg	8/29	
Krumau	12/111	
Kufstein	/98	
Küstrin	4/22	
Kulmbach	Stand. 89	
Landeshut	2/31	
Landsberg	5/22	
Landshut	5/90	
Landsweiler	8/81	
Langenberg	8/66	
Langensalza	10/44	
Lauban	8/32	
Laucha	10/37	Segelflugschule
Lauenburg	7/16	Flugmodellbauschule
Lauerberg	1/8	
Laufen	5/87	
Leibnitz	3/115	
Leipzig	Stand. 39, 1/39, 2/39	
Leitmeritz	17/40	
Leoben	4/115	
Leobschütz	4/29	
Leslau	5/120	
Liegnitz	1/32	
Lienz	4/113	
Linz/D	Stand. 111 1/111, 2/111	
Linz/Rhein	6/72	
Lippstadt	4/58	
Lissa	9/121	
Litzmannstadt	Stand. 119	
Loben (Lublinitz)	2/29	
Lötzen	7/2	
Lokstedt	10/15	
Ludenschein	3/58	
Ludwigshafen	2/81	
Lübbecke	9/60	
Lübeck	6/16	
Lüneburg	Stand. 18 1/18	
Lustenau	4/98	
Luxemburg	Stand. 78	
Lyck	9/2	
Magdeburg	Stand. 52, 1-2/52	
Mähr-Schönberg	8/33	
Mannheim	Stand. 79, 4/80	Flugzeugführerschule
Marburg/L	5/45	
Marienburg	6/3	

LOCATION	UNIT(S)	ESTABLISHMENTS
Marienburg-Sachsen		Segelflugschule
Marienehe	3/12	
Marktredwitz	9/89	
Mechtel	10/34	
Meiningen	4/44	
Meissen	8/38, 10/38	
Meissner, Hoher		Flugmodellbauschule
Melk	2/116	
Memel	14/1	
Merseburg	9/36	
Meschede	6/58	
Metz	Stand. 84	
Metz-süd	2/84	
Minden	5/60	
Moers	6/67	
Molsheim	9/83	
Mosbach	2/80	
Mülhausen	Stand. 82, 12/82	
Mülheim	Stand. 67	
Mülheim/Ruhr	2/67	
München	Stand. 94, 4/94, Stand. 97	Gr. 14-Hochland
München-Gladbach	5/66	Flugzeugführerschule
Münster im Westfalen	Stand. 59, 2/59	
Mürzzuschlag	6/115	
Myslowitz	7/34	
Naugard	1/10	
Naumburg	7/36	
Neheim	9/58	
Neisse	11/29	
Neumünster	Stand. 16	
Neuruppin	Stand. 24, 3/24	
Neuss	7/66	
Neustadt/Aisch	9/87	
Neustadt/Weinstr.	Stand 81	
Neustettin	2/8	
Neutitschein	3/33	
Neuwied	5/72	
Nikolai	4/35, 8/34	
Nikolsburg	11/116	
Norden	6/17	
Northeim	13/50	
Nürnberg	Stand. 87, 1/87	Gr. 13-Main-Donau
Oberhausen	4/67	
Oels	10/30	
Oerlinghausen in Lippe		Gr. 10-Westfalen
Offenbach/M	2/77, 2/78	
Offenburg	5/107	
Oldenburg	Stand. 17, 1/17	

LOCATION	UNIT(S)	ESTABLISHMENTS
Oppeln	Stand. 29	
Ortelsburg	4/2, 6/2	
Oschersleben	18/52	
Osnabrück	11/17	
Ostrowo	5/119	
Pabianice	4/119	
Paderborn	2/60	
Passau	4/90	
Peine	4/50	
Perleberg	1/24	
Pforzheim	8/80	
Pirmasens	4/81	
Plauen	12/37	
Plock	11/2	
Posen	Stand. 121	Gr. 5-Wartheland
Potsdam	Stand. 25	
Prag	18/40	
Preetz	12/16	
Pr. Holland	3/2, 4/3	
Prien	4/97	
Pr. Eylau	9/1	
Pyritz	3/10	
Radzionkau (Buchatz/Scharley)	12/34	
Rangsdorf		Reichsschule für Motorflugsport and Flugzeugführerschule
Rastatt	1/82, 1/83	
Rastenburg	5/2	
Ratibor	5/29, 1/35	
Recklinghausen	6/59	
Regensburg	Stand. 90, 1/90	Flugzeugführerschule
Reichenbach	8/31	
Reichenberg	2/40	
Remscheid	12/66	
Reutlingen	8/103	
Rheine	4/59	
Rhinow		Segelflugschule
Ribnitz	4/11	
Rosenheim	4/97	
Rossgarten		Wehrsportschule des NSFK
Rossitten		Segelflugschule
Rostock	2/12	
Rothenburg O. Tauber		Flugmodellbauschule
Rybnik	9/34, 3/35	
Rudolstadt	6/43	

LOCATION	UNIT(S)	ESTABLISHMENTS
Saalfeld	5/43	
Saarbrücken	10/81	
Saarburg	8/84	
Saargemünd	7/84	
Saarlautern	12/81	
St. Ingbert/Saar	6/81	
St. Veit	3/113	
Salzburg	Stand. 201, 1/201	
Salzgitter		Segelflugschule
Salzwedel	6/52	
Sangerhausen	6/36	
Scharley	8/34	
Schleiz	4/43	
Schlettstadt	11/83	
Schmalkalden	6/44	
Schneidemühl	Stand. 8, 5/8	
Schönfeld		Flugzeugführerschule
Schrobenhausen	12/94	
Schüren b. Eschede		Werkstattleiterschule Segelflugschule
Schwabach	6/87	
Schwäb. Gmünd	6/102	
Schwäb. Hall	2/102	
Schwandorf	3/90	
Schwangau		Segelflugschule
Schwenningen	Stand. 104, 9/104	
Schwerin	Stand. 12, 9/12	
Schwerte	7/57	
Schwientochlowitz		Segelfluglager
Selb	8/89	
Senftenberg	2/23	
Sensburg	5/2	Segelflugschule
Sieburg	4/65	
Siegen	7/58	
Singen	8/82	
Soldau	8/2	
Soldin	1/14	
Solingen	11/66	
Sonderhausen	12/44	
Sonneburg	1/44	
Sonthofen		Flugzeugführerschule
Sorau	8/23	
Spitzenberg		Segelflugschule
Spremberg	5/23	
Sprottau	4/32	
Stainach	5/115	
Stargard	2/10	
Starnberg	9/94	
Stassfurt	7/53	
Steinberg		Segelflugschule
Stendal	7/52	
Sternberg	5/33	
Stettin	Stand. 10, 5-8/10	Gr. 2-Ostsee
Steyr	7/111	

LOCATION	UNIT(S)	ESTABLISHMENTS
Stockerau	9/116	
Stockstadt/M	5/77	
Stralsund	Stand. 11, 2/11	
Strassburg	Stand. 83, 7/83, 8/83	Gr. 16-Südwest
Straubing	2/90	
Strehlen	8/30	
Stuttgart	Stand. 101	Gr. 15-Schwaben
Sulzbach	9/81	
Swinemünde	10/10	
Tann	10/82	
Tarnowitz	1/34	
Taucha	5/39	
Telgte	3/59	
Teplitz-Schönau	Stand. 40,	
Teschen	17/40	
Thorn	2/126	
Tilsit	8/1	Flugzeugführerschule
Tilsit-Waldhof	4/3	
Torgau	10/36	
Traben-Trarbach	4/72	
Traunstein	5/97	
Trebbin		Versuchstelle des NSFK Segelflugschule
Trier	3/72	
Troppau	2/33	
Tübingen	7/101	
Ütersen	9/16	
Ulm	6/103	
Vacha	5/44	
Vechta	8/17	
Villach	6/113	
Vogelsang		Flugzeugführerschule
Wachtersberg		Segelflugschule
Waldenburg	3/31	
Walsrode	3/18, 5/18	
Waltershausen	7/44	
Wandsbeck	3/15	

LOCATION	UNIT(S)	ESTABLISHMENT
Wanne	4/61	
Wanne-Eickel	4/57	
Waren	9/11	
Warnemünde	4/12	
Warnsdorf	3/40	
Wasserkuppe		Segelflugschule
Weiden	11/89	
Weilheim an d. Teck		Segelflugschule
Weimar	Stand.43, 10/43	
Weissenburg	7/87	
Weiswasser	5/32	
Wels	III/2/111	
Wernigerode	11/53	
Wetzlar	7/75	
Wien	Stand.112,116 4/112,10/112 12/112	Gr. 17-Donau-Alpenland
Wien Mödling	6/112	
Wiener Neustadt	6/112	
Wiesbaden	11/75	
Wiesen/Siegkreis	6/72	
Wildbad	4/101	
Wilhelmsburg	4/116	
Wilhelmshafen	5/17	
Wippenfürth	5/65	
Wittenberg	11/36	
Wittlich	6/78	
Wolfratshausen	1/97	
Würzburg	Stand.88,1/88, 3/88,7/88	
Wuppertal	9/66,10/66	
Zabern	5/83	
Zeitz	8/36	
Zell am See		Segelflugschule
Zella-Mehlis	3/44	
Zempelburg	3/126	
Zittau	6/38	
Znaim	Stand.114 12/116	
Zossen	7/25	
Zuackenbrück	10/17	
Zwickau	9/37	
Zwittau	10/33	

CONFIDENTIAL

SUPREME HEADQUARTERS ALLIED EXPEDITIONARY FORCE
EVALUATION AND DISSEMINATION SECTION
G-2 (COUNTER INTELLIGENCE SUB-DIVISION)

B-A-S-I-C   H-A-N-D-B-O-O-K

THE NSFK

(Das Nationalsozialistische Fliegerkorps)

NATIONAL SOCIALIST AVIATION

CORPS

ANNEXE D:

WHO'S WHO IN THE NSFK

	Page
Key	D1
Abbreviations used in the WHO'S WHO	D2
WHO'S WHO	D4

This Annexe should be inserted in the publication E.D.S./G/2, and the Table of contents amended accordingly.

E.D.S./G/2
Compiled by MIRS (LONDON Branch)
From Material Available at
WASHINGTON and LONDON

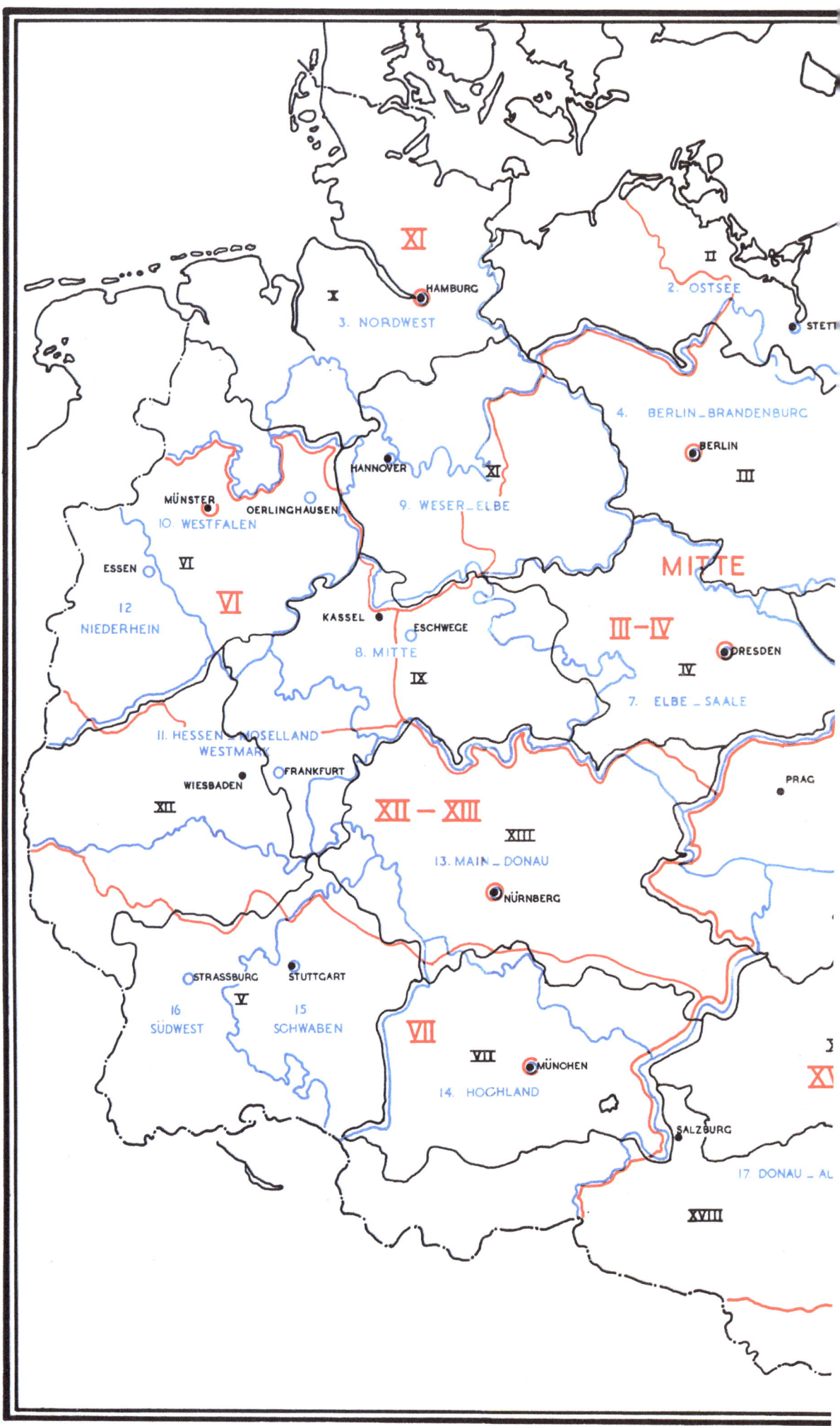

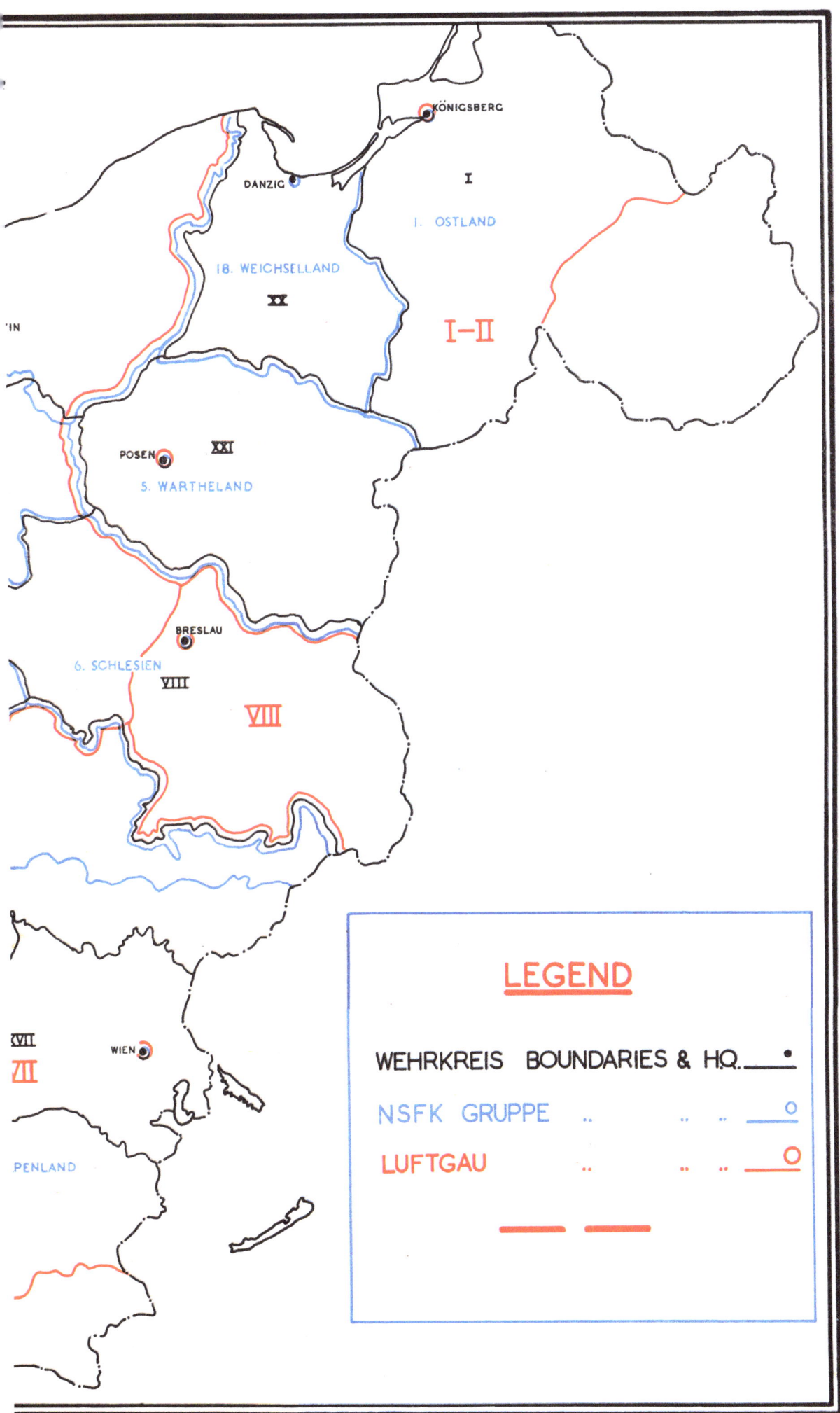

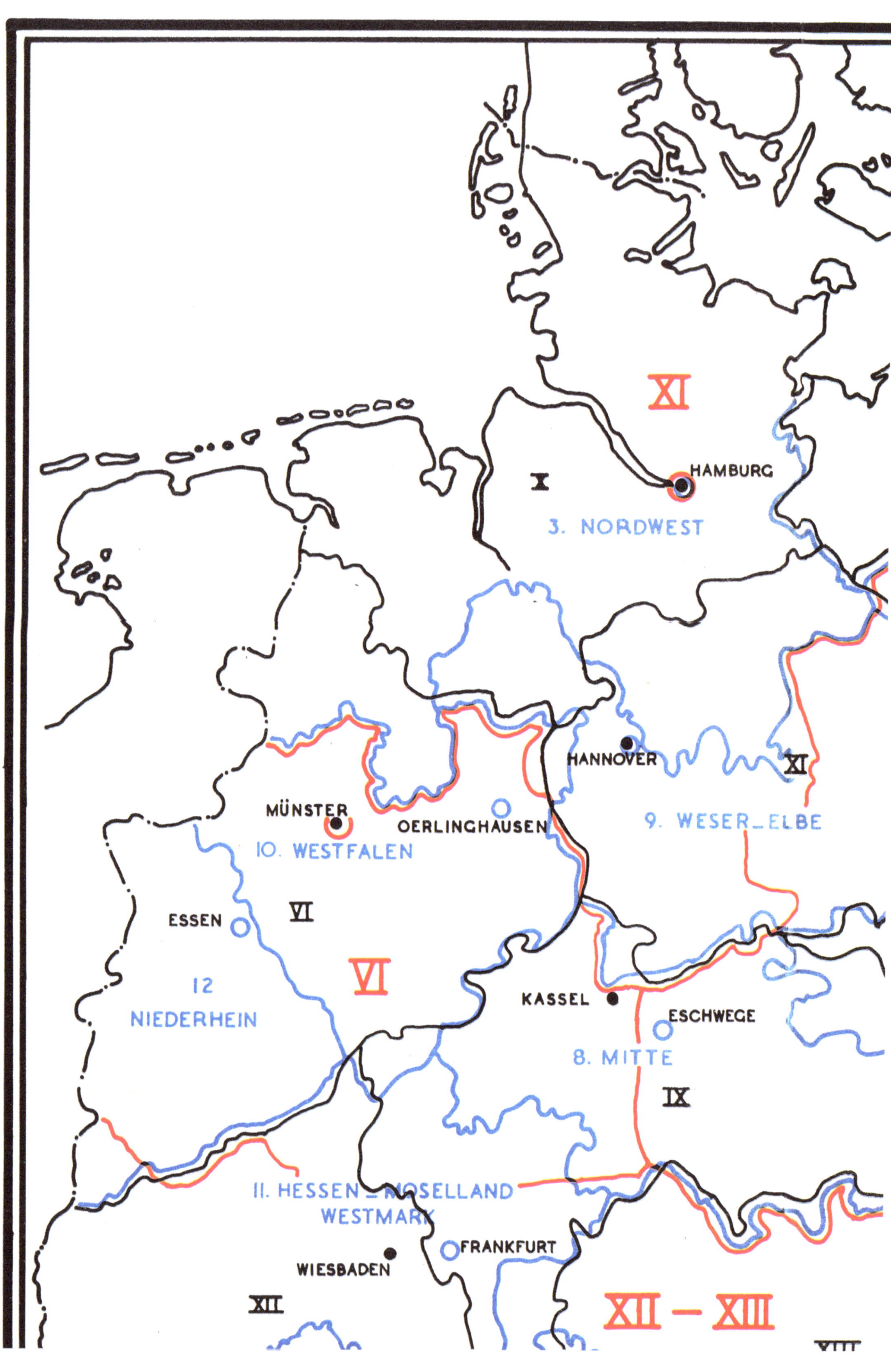

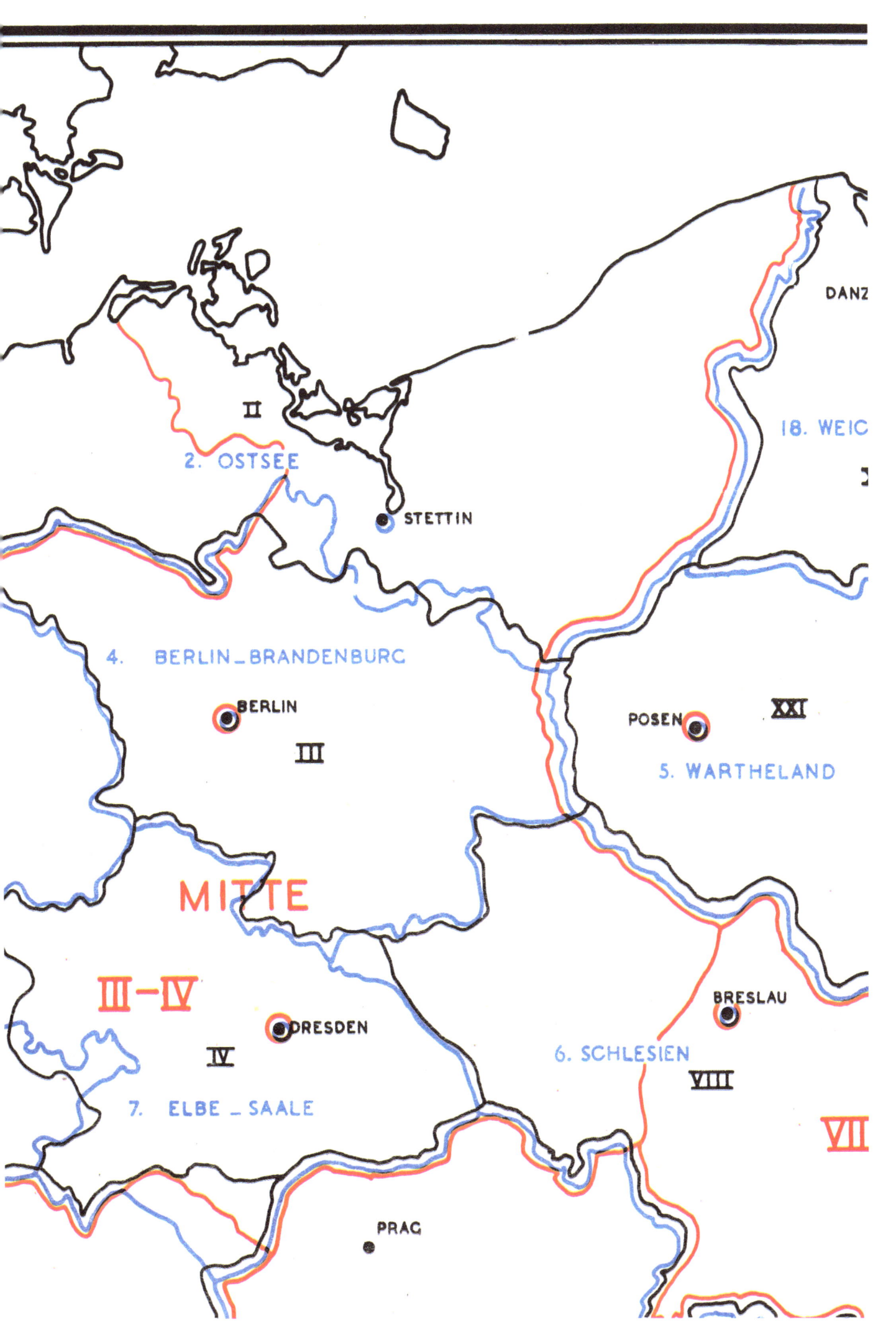

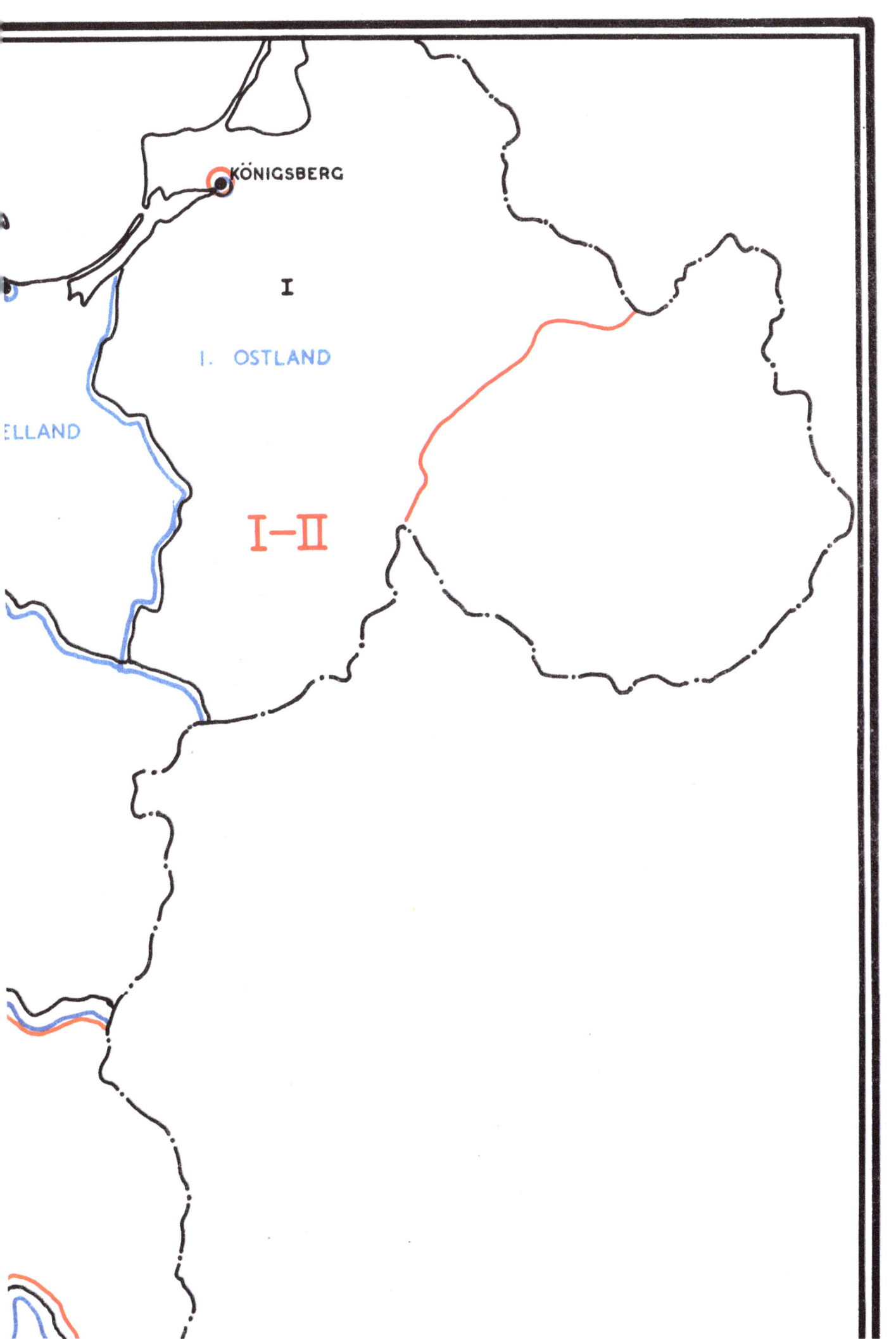

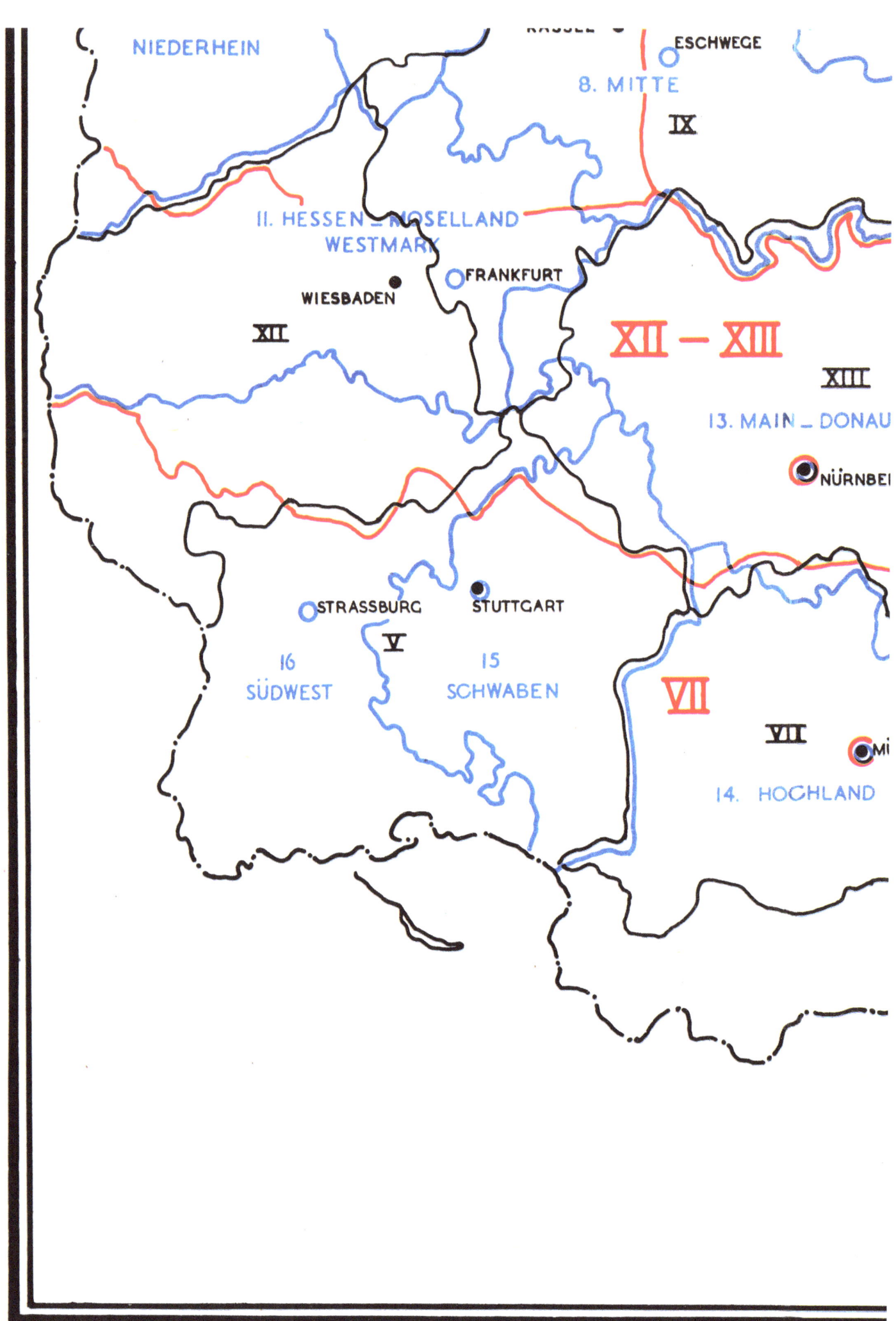

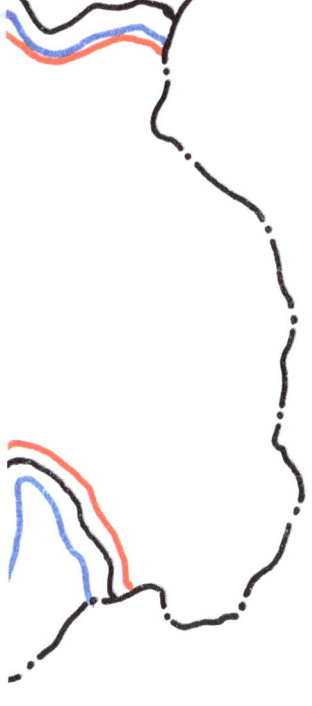

LEGEND

WEHRKREIS BOUNDARIES & H.Q. —·

NSFK GRUPPE .. .. ..—o

LUFTGAU .. .. ..—o

KEY

1. The attempt has been made to list in alphabetical order all identified personalities holding officer's, especially senior officer's rank, in the NSFK. The list cannot be regarded as complete.

2. Ranks held and posts filled are not always certain beyond any doubt and two persons may be found entered as holding the identical post or command.
    This is partly due to undated source material and partly due to the fact that transfers as well as promotions are frequent and information on them is not always available.
    Reference should be made for commanders etc. of units to the Order of Battle in Annexe A, which will in some cases conflict with information in the WHO'S WHO.

3. German titles, ranks and designations have been retained in most cases. Only in some cases could an approximate translated version be given. Any attempt to translate all German terms would have resulted in misinterpretation.
    Reference should be made for translations, to standard publications, including the EDS/G series, and the EDS CI Handbook for Germany, which contains an abbreviations glossary.

4. Dates shown in parentheses indicate the date of source material, when the latter was available.
    Following rank designations, dates indicate time of promotion, or award of seniority.

5. A list of abbreviations used in the WHO'S WHO is given for convenience in this Annexe.

6. For purposes of alphabetical listing the normal German usage has been followed, of treating the modified vowels ä, ö, ü as though spelt ae, oe, ue: thus for example ä immediately precedes af.

ABBREVIATIONS USED IN THE WHO'S WHO

ABBREVIATION	GERMAN EQUIVALENT	APPROXIMATE ENGLISH EQUIVALENT
Abt.	Abteilung	Department, bureau office.
akt	aktiv(- er, etc)	active
BF	Brigadeführer	Generalmajor
bes.	besonder(-en, etc)	special
d.	der, die, das, des, dem, den.	the, of the, to the, for the.
dt.	deutsch(-e/er/es, etc.)	German
Dr.	Doktor	doctor
Frhr	Freiherr	Baron
Gen	General	General
GF	Gruppenführer	Generalleutnant
Gr.	Gruppe	Group Command (HQ)
Hstuf	Hauptsturmführer	Captain
K	Kommandeur/Kommandierender	Commander/Commanding
Korpsf	Korpsführer	NSFK Commander-in-Chief.
LW	Luftwaffe	Airforce
Mdr	Mitglied des Reichstages	Member of the Reichstages
MdVGH	Mitglied des Volksgerichtshofes	Member of the People's Court.
NSFK	Nationsozialistisches Fliegerkorps	National Aviation Flying Corps
OF	Oberführer	Sr. Col.
OGF	Obergruppenführer	General
OSBF	Obersturmbannführer	Lt. Col.
Ostuf	Obersturmführer	1st. Lt.
Präs	Präsident	President
Prof	Professor	Professor

SBF	Sturmbannführer	Major
San	Sanitäts	Medical
SF	Standartenführer	
St.	Sturm	Coy
Stellv	Stellvertretender	Deputy
Str	Strasse	Street
Stuf	Sturmführer	2nd. Lt.
z.Zt	zur Zeit	at present (i.e. usually means "at the date of the source of information")

BASTGEN, Wendel   BF

    In Operational Office at BERLIN (Führungsamt BERLIN, Abt. VI)
    Chief of Training (Chef. d. Ausbildungsamtes)
    Leader of the Personnel Office (Leiter d.Personalabt.)

BAUER   SBF

    Commander of Standarte 12
    HQ: SCHWERIN

BEINES, Alfred   SBF

    Chief of Staff Gr. 12 NIEDERRHEIN

BELONOSCHKIN, Dr.   San.Ostuf

    Gruppenarzt WARTHELAND

BENGSCH   SF

    In Operational Bureau at BERLIN (Führungsamt BERLIN)
    Section II Model Aviation (Abt.II Modellflug)
    Chief of Model Aviation in H.Q. (Leiter d. Abt. Modellflug in d. Korpsführung)

BERTRAM   SF

    Commander of Standarte 37
    HQ: CHEMNITZ

BLESSIN   Hstuf

    Technical Chief for wireless training (Sachgebiets-
    leiter für d. NSFK Gr. 15 WÜRTTEMBERG)

BODENER, Max   SF

    Principal of the Nat. Academy for Aviation (Leiter d. Reichsschule für fliegerische Ausbildung)

BRAND   SF

    Commander of Standarte 125 or 126 (DANZIG or BROMBERG)

BRAUN, Carl   OGF (20/4/41)

    Commander of Gr. 14 HOCHLAND until 1/5/40
    Kommandeur einer Fliegerschule d. L.W. to 1/5/42
    Oberst d. L.W.

BRINKMANN, Friedrich Georg GF (20/4/43)

    Commander of Gr. 6 SCHLESIEN

BÜLOW, Harry v.   OGF

    Inspekteur d. NSFK
    Oberst d. Wehrluftwaffe
    Landwirt
    Born: 19/11/1897

C

CHRISTIANSEN, Friedrich

    Gen. d. Flieger
    Former Militärbefehlshaber in HOLLAND
    MdVGH

CRONEISS   GF

    Commander of Gr. 13 MAIN-DONAU
    HQ: NÜRNBERG, O - Theodorstr. 1.

CRONEISZ, Carl   GF

    Commander of Gr. 13
    MdR
    Born: 9/1/1891

D

__DAMRAU__ SF

> SD in INNSBRUCK
> President of the State Postal Directorate (Präs. d. Reichspostdirektion: INNSBRUCK)

__DESCHER__ SF

> Commander of Standarte 35
> HQ: BIELITZ

__DITTRICH__ OF

> Commander of Standarte 40
> HQ: PRAG

__DITTRICH__ SF

> Commander of Standarte 40
> HQ: TEPLITZ-SCHÖNAU

__DRESSKER__ Ostuf

KIEL (13/3/44)

E

EICHHORN, Max SF

    In Operational Office BERLIN (Führungsamt)
    Chief of Technical Bureau III at H.Q. (Leiter d.
    Abt. III für Technik in d. Korpsführung)

ENGEL, Dr. Hans OF

    Ministerial Director in the Ministry of Labour
    (Ministerial-direktor im Arbeitsministerium)
    Secretary of State (Staatssekretär 9/3/42)
    Chief of Department II in the Ministry of Labour
    (Leiter d.Hpt.amts II in Reichsarbeitsministerium)
    Born: 17/11/1887

ERBACHER GF

    Commander of Gr. 15 SCHWABEN
    HQ: STUTTGART, Neckarstr. 195

ESCHWEGE, Elmar v. OGF

    Commander of Gr. 8
    Oberstleutnant d. Flieger
    Born: AUE, ESCHWEGE 7/5/1896

FIESELER, Gerhard   OF

    In aircraft production, industrialist
    (Flugzeugindustrieller)
    Wehrwirtschaftsführer

FISCHER   OBSF

    Commander of Standarte 38
    HQ: DRESDEN

FLEBBE   GF SF(?)

    Commander of Gr. 14. HOCHLAND
    HQ: MÜNCHEN, Theresienstr. 84

FRIEDEL   OSBF

    Commander of Standarte 53
    HQ: DESSAU
    Deputy Commander of Standarte 52 MAGDEBURG

FRITSCH   SF

    Possibly Commanding Officer of the Nat. Glider
    School (Kommandant d. Reichssegelfliegerschule)
    SPITZBERG

FRODIEN, Friedr. Wilhelm   GF

    Commander of Gr. 2
    Flugleiter bei du. Lufthansa 1938
    Chef d. Personalämter im Stab d. Korpsführung
    Born: 30/8/1897

FUNK   SBF

    Specialist (Sachbearbeiter in Gr. 14)

G

GEEIGNTER　　　　　　　　SF

　　" MÜNCHEN
　　(may be same as below)

GEIGNETTER　　　　　　　Ostuf

　　Commander of Standarte 98
　　HQ: INNSBRUCK
　　(may be same as above)

GLEISNER, Arno　　　　　OF SF (?) (22/5/43)

　　Commander of Gr. 16 SÜDWEST
　　HQ: STRASSBURG, Schwarzwaldstr. 26

GODT, Walter　　　　　　GF (20/4/43)

　　Commander of Gr. 12 NIEDERRHEIN
　　HQ: ESSEN, Alfredstr. 61-63
　　formerly Führer d. Gr. 13

GÖPFERT, Arthur　　　　 OF

　　Leiter d Volksbildungsministeriums SACHSEN
　　MdR
　　Ministerialrat
　　Born: 7/6/1902

GONNERT, Dr. Fritz　　　GF (20/4/43)

GRAF　　　　　　　　　　Ostuf

　　Commander of Standarte 90 REGENSBURG

GRAMBOW　　　　　　　　 OF SF (?)

　　Commander of Gr. 4 BERLIN-BRANDENBURG
　　HQ: BERLIN, Meier-Otto-Str. 8/9

GREISER, Arthur

    Gauleiter and Reichstatthalter of WARTHELAND
    MdR
    Gaujägermeister WARTHELAND
    Born: 22/1/97
    Address: POSEN, Königsring 5

GROHER   OF SF(?)

    Commander of Gr. 13 MAIN-DONAU
    HQ: NÜRNBERG O, Theresienstr. 1

H

HAASE, Ernst Günther   Hstuf

   Leiter d. Erprobungsstelle TREBBIN (29/11/42)

HARIG

   Commander of Gr. 16 Standarte 85
   HQ: METZ

HAUSEN, Frhr, Heino v.   SF

   Stabsarbeiter d. Standarte 94 MÜNCHEN
   MÜNCHEN, Mühlbauerstr. 5

HEINKELL, Dr. Ernst   OF

   Director of the Heinkel Works (Leiter d. Heinkellwerke)

HIDESSEN, Ferdinand v.   GF

   Commander of Gr. 16 SÜDWEST
   HQ: STRASSBURG, Schwarzwaldstr. 26
   Formerly active officer
   First German Flier over PARIS 1914
   1933-38 Polizeipräsident of WALDENBURG
   1933 MdR
   Born: 1887 MINDEN, Westfalen

HINZ   OSBF

   Commander of Standarte 36
   HQ: HALLE, S.

HISZ, Mathias   GF

HOCHREINER, Roland   SF

   Commander of Standarte 98, INNSBRUCK

HOECKRICH, Kurt   Ostuf

   Head of the Glider Section
   (Leiter d.Abt.Segelflug im Stabe d. NSFK Brigade
    21 WEICHSEL)
   DANZIG am Holzraum 4

HOEFERER, OF

    In d. Gr. BAYREUTH 13

HOPSTOCK SF

    In WARNEMÜNDE

HOTH OSBF

    Commander of Standarte 11
    HQ: STRALSUND

HOTH OSBF

    Führer zur bes. Verwendung d. Gr. 2 STETTIN

HUPFAUF Hstuf

    Commander of Standarte 89
    HQ: KULMBACH

HUPFAUF Ostuf

    Commander of Standarte 89 COBURG (27/3/44)

J

JACHTMANN, Ernst

    Specialist for gliding (Sachgebietsleiter für Segelflug in d. LUFTHANSA)

JUHRE　　　　　　　　SHF

    Pressassistant to H.Q. (Pressereferent d. Korpsführung NSFK)

K

KAPONIG, Sepp　　　　　　Ostuf

　　Stabsbearbeiter und Adjutant d. Standarte 113
　　　　　　　　　　　　　　KLAGENFURT

KASSEL　　　　　　　　　　OF

KEHRSBERG, Arno　　　　　GF

　　Commander of Gr. 5 WARTHELAND (23/3/44)
　　HQ: POSEN, Tiergartenstr. 6.

KEHRBERG, Arno　　　　　　BF

　　In Operational Office (Im Führungsamt)
　　Address: BERLIN, W.51, Meier-Otto-Str. 8-9.

KELLER, Alfred　　　　　　Korpsf.

　　Generaloberst (28/7/43)
　　Born: 19/9/1882

KELLNER　　　　　　　　　OF

　　Commander of Gr. 15 WÜRTTEMBERG, 14
　　Address: KIRCHHEIM

KELLNER,　　　　　　　　 SF (?)

　　Commander of Gr. 15 SCHWABEN
　　HQ: STUTTGART, Neckarstr. 195

KEMPE, Friedr.-Karl　　　SF

　　At present in LUXEMBOURG
　　Address: NEURUPPIN, Steinstr. 120

KITTNER　　　　　　　　　Hstuf

　　Commander of Standarte 75
　　HQ: FRANKFURT/Main

KNOTHE   San.OF

    Address: BERLIN

KODERLE, Dr. Richard   OF

    SALZBURG
    1938: Gauamtsleiter: BERLIN
    Reichsredner
    Gauinspekteur: STEIERMARK
    Born: 25/9/1889

KÖPPNER, Willmar   OF

KÖRNER, Dr. Erich   OF

    Chief of Personnel Section of the Nat. Post
    Office IV (Leiter d. Personalabt. d. Reichspost IV)
    Fachamtsleiter (Post) im RDB
    Oberbereichsleiter (NSDAP)
    Formerly President of the Nat. Postal System BERLIN
    (Früherer Reichspostpräsident: BERLIN)

KRAFT, Hubert   SF

    MdR
    Reichsredner
    Ministerialrat   "
    Kreisamtsleiter: MUHLHAUSEN, Baden

KRATZ, Dr. Erwin   GF

    Commander of Gr. 9 WESER-ELBE
    HQ: HANNOVER, Waldenseestr. 1
    Born: 26/6/1891

KRUGER, Albert   GF

    Commander of Gr. 17 DONAU-ALPENLAND (31/3/40)
    HQ: WIEN III, Metternichweg 6

KUBLITZ   ?

    Stabsleiter d. Korpsführung since 23/3/44
    Chief of Operations Bureau (Chef d. Führungsamtes)
    Address: POSEN

KUNZ OF

    Chief of Glider Section at Operational HQ of NSFK
    High Command. (Leiter d. Segelflugabt. in d.
    Korpsführung)
    St. Leiter d. Führungsamtes in Vertretung d. Amtes
    Ausbildung.

KUSSTATSCHER SBF

    Commander of Standarte 98 INNSBRUCK (?)
    Now at the front

L

LANGE, Dr. Kurt   BF

>Chief of Section for Financial questions in the
Ministry of Economics. (Leiter d. Abt. für
Finanzfragen im Wirtschaftsministerium)
Vice President of the Reichsbank (Vicepräsident d.
Reichsbank)
Ministerialdirektor
MdR
Vizepräsident d. dt. Gold-Diskont Bank
Born: 8/7/1885 EISENACH
Address: BERLIN-Dahlem, Vogelsang 15

LEDY   SF

>In Operational Office: BERLIN (Im Führungsamt:BERLIN)
Abt. V
Military Sports Training and Indoctrination (Wehrsport
und Weltanschaung)

LEHN   OSBF

>Commander of Standarte 57

LEHSTEN, Wilhelm   OSBF

>Commander of Standarte 119
HQ: LITZMANNSTADT
Address: Leo-Schlageterstr. 95

LENTZ   Hstuf

>Commander of the Glider School:
SCHWANGAU (Leiter der Segelflugschule)

LOERZE, Bruno   OGF

D17

M

MAGER   Stuf

    Garrison Commander of the Hitler Youth, appointed for the duration (K-Standortführer d. H.J. - (Schwerte))

MARSEN

    Referent im Stab d. Gr. 9 für Segelflug

MEYER, Heinrich

    Gruppenarzt 7 SACHSEN
    Chief of Medical Association: SACHSEN (Leiter d. Arztkammer: SACHSEN)

MEYER, Paul   SBF

    Commander of Standarte 82
    HQ: MÜLHAUSEN

MIEMAN (NIEMANN?)   Hstuf

    Commander of Standarte 121, POSEN

MILBERT   OSBF

    Commander of Standarte 16
    HQ: NEUMÜNSTER

MOLITOR, v   GF

    Commander of Gr. 11 MOSELLAND-HESSEN WESTMARK
    HQ: FRANKFURT/Main, Fellnerstr. 5.
    Born: 23/8/1895

MÜLLER-KLINGSPOR   SF

    Commander of Standarte 112
    HQ: VIENNA

MUNNICHOW   Stuf

    Leiter der Aussenstelle RADOM d. NSFK

N

NAUJOKS   OF

     Deputy Commander of Gr. 2 OSTSEE
     HQ: STETTIN, Arndstr. 28

NEUHAUSEN, Dr. Franz   OGF

     Consul General in BELGRAD
     Chief of Military Admin. South East (Chef d.
      Militärverwaltung Südost)
     (Generalbevollmächtigter für d. Metallersatzbau
      Südost im Vierjahresplan)
     Chairman of the Control Board for the Allgemeine
      Jugoslavische Bankverein (Vorsitzender d. Auf-
      sichtsrats d. Allg. Jugosl. Bankvereins)
     Born: 13/12/1887

NIEMANN (MIEMAN?)   Hstuf

     Commander of Standarte 121
     HQ: POSEN

O

OBERSTE-LEHN, Hermann   SF

    Commander of Standarte 57 DORTMUND

OHNESORGE, Dr. Wilhelm   OGF

    Reichs Post Minister (a cabinet Member)
    Born: 1872

OPPERMANN   OGF

    Commander of Gr. 1 OSTLAND
    HQ: KÖNIGSBERG/Preussen, Gen. Litzmannstr. 21/25

OPPERMANN, Ewald   OGF

    Generalkommissar NIKOLAJEW
    MdR
    Gaurichter: OSTPREUSSEN
    Maurer und Zimmermeister (as listed officially
     under profession)
    Born: 25/2/1896 KÖNIGSBERG
    Address: HANNOVER-Kirchrode, Ostfeldestr. 33

P

PETSCHELT OSBF

Leiter d. Abt. Funk und Unterricht d. Korpsführung (25/1/44)

PICKHAN, Prof. San.-BF

POPP OSBF

Commander of Standarte 39
HQ: LEIPZIG

R

REINHOLD SF

HQ: HAMBURG

RHEINHOLD OF

Deputy Commander of Gr. 3. NORDWEST
HQ: HAMBURG 13, Oberfeldstr. 17

REISCHOLD SF

Deputy Commander of Gr. 3 NORDWEST, HAMBURG

RICHTHOFEN, Frhr. Bolko v. SF

Born: 16/4/1903
Address: BERLIN, Schmagendorf, Davoserstr. 4

ROITH-MEYER Hstuf.

Commander of Standarte 87
HQ: NÜRNBERG

RÖSCHMANN Hstuf.

(20/9/43)

RUDL Hstuf.

Commander of 2. Standarte 113
HQ: KLAGENFURT

S

SAUKE, Karl OGF

Temporarily Deputy C-in-C and COS, Cmdr. of the combined Group 2 and 4 (z.Zt. Stellv. d. Korpsführers und Chef d. Stabes, Führer d. Vereinigten Gr. 2 und 4 BERLIN und POMMERN)

SASSMANNSHAUSEN SF

Commander of Standarte 34 KATTOWITZ

SCHÄFER OSBF

Commander of Standarte 32
HQ: LIEGNITZ

SCHNELL, Prof.Dr. San.-BF

SCHOPPE, Dr. SF

SCHRÖDER, Wilhelm GF

Chief of Admin. Bureau of the NSFK (Chef d. Verwaltungsamtes d. NSFK)
Born: 1898

SCHULZE-HULBE Hstuf.

Commander of Standarte 116

SCHUMACHER OSBF

Commander of Standarte 103 STUTTGART
HQ: FRIEDRICHSHAFEN

SCHWARZGRUBER SF

Commander of Standarte 3
HQ: ELBING

SEEL, Hans   OF

    Ministerialdirigent im Innenministerium
    Leiter d. Unterabt. in d. Abt. II

SEETZEN, Heinz   SF

SEIBRANDT   OF

    In STRASSBURG

SELLING   OF

    Commander of Gr. 18 WEICHSELLAND
    Formerly NSFK Brigade 125 DANZIG
    HQ: DANZIG
    Address: Schickaugasse 6

SIELER   GF

    Commander of Gr. 4 BERLIN-Brandenburg
    HQ: BERLIN, Meier-Ottostr. 8/9
    (may be same as below)

SIELER, Heinrich   GF

    In KOBLENZ (4/44)
    Born: 26/11/1893
    (may be same as above)

SIEVERT   OSBF

    Sachgebietsleiter d. Gr. IV BERLIN-Brandenburg
    Commander of Standarte 26 or 27 BERLIN

SIMMER, Fritz   BF

SOMMICHSEN   OF

    Chief of Central Section (Leiter d. Zentralab-
    teilung)

SPORLEDER, Gerhard   OG

    Commander of Gr. 6 SCHLESIEN
    HQ: BRESLAU, Hindenburgplatz 4

STAMER   SF

STEINER, Richard   Stuf.

    On the Staff of Gruppe I
    At present Unteroffizier in d. Wehrluftwaffe
    Deutsches Kreuz in Gold

T

THIELE　　　　　　　　　SF

    Liaison officer for the Reichspostministerium
     (Verbindungsoffizier d. Reichspostministeriums)
    At present NSKK Amtsmann (12/42)

THOMSEN, Otto　　　　　　OF

    In Operational Bureau BERLIN (Führungsamt
    BERLIN, Abt. IV)
    Leiter d. Abt. Motor und Ballonflug
    Inspekteur d. Motorflugschulen

U

ULRICH   SHF

     Commander of Standarte 31 FRANKENSTEIN

ULBRICHT   SF

     SUDETENLAND

ULRICH   OSBF

     Commander of Standarte 29 SCHLESIEN

V

VERGENZ, Erich   SF

　　　In d. Reichssegelflugschule
　　　Holder of the world record in gliding
　　　Address: WIEN

W

WESTERKAMP

    Hauptreferent für Film, Bild, Unterricht

WITTENBECHER   Ostuf.

    Commander of Segelflugschule SCHWANGAU

WOLF   SF

    Chief of Staff of Gr. 9 WESNER-ELBE
    HQ: HANNOVER, Walderseestr. 1

WOLF   OF

    Commander of Gr. 18, WEICHSEL, DANZIG
    Member of General Gouvernment

WÖLL, Ullrich   SF

    Commander of Standarte 29
    HQ: OPPELN

WÖLL   Hstuf

    Commander of Standarte 30 BRESLAU

Z

ZAHN, Werner   GF

>Commander of Gr. 3
>Born: 25/11/1897
>Address: KARLSRUHE, Leopoldplatz 72

ZAHN   GF

>Commander of Gr. 3 NORDWEST
>HQ: HAMBURG 13, Oberfelderstr. 17

ZIMMERMANN, Dr.   GF

>Commander of Gr. 7 ELBE-SAALE
>HQ: DRESDEN A, Kreutzerstr. 21

ZOLFEL

>Referent für Funk und Unterricht in d. Korpsführung

CONFIDENTIAL

SUPREME HEADQUARTERS ALLIED EXPEDITIONARY FORCE
EVALUATION AND DISSEMINATION SECTION
G-2 (Counter Intelligence Sub-Division)

B-A-S-I-C H-A-N-D-B-O-O-K

THE NSFK

(Das Nationalsozialistische Fliegerkorps)

NATIONAL SOCIALIST AVIATION CORPS

A N N E X E   E

Captured Order of Battle (1940, with amendments)
of the NSFK

1. This Annexe is intended as supplementary information to the Order of Battle already published (and revised) as Annexe A.

2. Whereas Annexe A was compiled from various sources and from information of various dates, Annexe E represents a complete Order of Battle (Anschriftenverzeichnis) as published by the Germans in 1940, and amended by them at later dates unknown.

3. The relevant parts of the document have been reproduced almost exactly (i.e. subject to certain translations and changes in layout) and no attempt has been made to combine it with the information contained in Annexe A, since the value of its completeness and definite date would thereby be lost.

4. It will be seen that in many cases Annexe E fills in gaps in the Order of Battle given in Annexe A. Where the two Annexes conflict on the subject of location, all such locations should be taken as possible variants.

5. It was considered useful to show the original entries as well as all subsequent alterations made by the Germans. These deleted entries have been shown, usually preceded by the word "formerly". This, includes cases where the Germans made more than one amendment to the same entry. Again the word "formerly" sometimes indicates an entry which was deleted but for which no new entry was substituted. In other cases the use of a footnote, or of the word "deleted", in parentheses, will indicate clearly the German amendment.

6. Only a few translations, usually in column headings, have been made; most of the terms used have already been translated in the remainder of the book.

E.D.S./G/2 (Amdt.No.3)   April 1945

CONFIDENTIAL

GRUPPE 1 (Ostland)

Headquarters: Königsberg/Preussen
General-Litzmann-Strasse 21/25
Tel: 24071

Flugzeugführerschule Tilsit
    Flugplatz Weynothen
    Tel: 3259
    Bahnstation: Tilsit

Flugzeugführerschule Allenstein
    Flugplatz Deuthen
    Tel: 2492
    Bahnstation: Allenstein

Flugzeugführerschule Königsberg
    Flugplatz Devau, Halle 4
    Tel: 37257
    Bahnstation: Königsberg/Pr.
                  Rothenstein Güterbhf.

Reichssegelflugschule Rossitten
    Kur. Nehrung
    Tel: Rossitten 13
    Bahnstation: Granz/Ostpr.

Segelflugschule Sensburg/Ostpr.
    Tel: Sensburg 289
    Bahnstation: Sensburg/Ostpr.

STANDARTE NO.	HQ LOCATION	COMPONENT UNITS - (STÜRME)	
1	Königsberg/Pr. General-Litzmannstr. (21/25 Tel: 24071 formerly Hintertragheim 18 Tel: 32 154	1/1 2/1 3/1 4/1 5/1 6/1 7/1 8/1 9/1 10/1 11/1 12/1	Königsberg Königsberg Königsberg Königsberg-Land Pillau formerly: Palmnicken Neukuhren Heiligenbeil Braunsberg Pr. Eylau Bartenstein Gerdauen Tapiau

CONFIDENTIAL

CONFIDENTIAL

GRUPPE 1 (contd.)

STANDARTE NO.	HQ LOCATION	COMPONENTS UNITS - STÜRME)	

2	Allenstein
	Schlossgarten
	Tel: 3165
		1/2
		2/2
		3/2
		4/2
		5/2
		6/2
		7/2
		*8/2
		*9/2
		
		*10/2
		
		*11/2
			Allenstein
			Osterode
			Pr. Holland
			Heilsberg
			Sensburg
			Ortelsburg
			Lötzen
			Soldau
			Zichenau
			  formerly: Mielau
			Mackeim
			  formerly: Praschnitz
			Schröttersburg
			  formerly: Plock

3	Gumbinnen Strasse am Güterbahnhof	1/3 2/3 3/3 4/3 5/3 6/3 7/3	Gumbinnen Memel Heydekrug Tilsit Insterburg Goldap Lyck

* Entries marked thus were added, as amendments, in the German original.

CONFIDENTIAL

CONFIDENTIAL

GRUPPE 2 (Ostsee) (formerly Nord)

Headquarters: Stettin
Arndtstrasse 28
Tel: 25171

Motorflugzeugführerschule Schönfeld
An der Ordensburg Krössinsee,
Schönfeld über Post Märk. Friedland
Tel: Märkisch Friedland 335/36
Bahnstation: Virchow, Abstellgleis Schönfeld

STANDARTE NO.	HQ LOCATION	COMPONENT UNITS (STÜRME)	
8	Neustettin Augustastr. 4 Tel: 545 formerly Julius Schreck Str. 4 Tel: 605	1/8 2/8 3/8 4/8 5/8 6/8 7/8 8/8 9/8 10/8 11/8 12/8	Lauenburg Bütow Stolp Schlochau Schneidemühl Schlawe Köslin Neustettin Dt. Krone Kolberg Belgard Dramburg
10	Stettin Langestr. 54 Tel: 27530 formerly Arndtstr. 28 Tel: 25171 formerly Falkenwalder Str. 128 Tel: 23547	1/10 2/10 3/10 4/10 5/10 6/10 7/10 8/10 9/10 10/10 11/10 12/10 13/10 14/10	Naugard Stargard Pyritz Cammin Stettin Stettin Stettin Stettin-Randow Greifenhagen Swinemünde Pasewalk Labes formerly: Regenwalde Greifenberg Friedeberg
11	Stralsund Heiligegeiststr. 76 Tel: 2923	1/11 2/11 3/11 4/11 5/11 6/11 7/11 8/11 9/11 10/11	Bergen auf Rügen Stralsund Greifswald Ribnitz Anklam Demmin Rechlin Neubrandenburg Waren Fürstenberg

CONFIDENTIAL

CONFIDENTIAL

GRUPPE 2 (Ostsee) (contd.)

STANDARTE NO.	HQ LOCATION	COMPONENT UNITS (STÜRME)	
12	Schwerin i. Mecklbg. Körnerstr. 22 formerly Adolf-Hitler-Str. 162 Tel: 3909	1/12 2/12 3/12 4/12 5/12 6/12 7/12 8/12 9/12 10/12	Güstrow Rostock Marienehe Warnemünde Parchim Festung Dömitz Wismar Tarnewitz Schwerin Boitzenburg

CONFIDENTIAL

GRUPPE 3 (Nordwest)

Headquarters: Hamburg 13 (formerly 37)
Oderfelderstr. 17
Tel: 521041/45

Flugzeugführerschule Hamburg Fuhlsbüttel,
    Flughafen, Halle A
    Tel: 595541. App 275
    Güterbahnhof: Hamburg Ohlsdorf
    (Deleted in original)

Technische Schule Hamburg-Wandsbek
    Holstenhof
    Tel: 287068

Reichsmodellflugschule (formerly Flugmodellbauschule),
    Lauenburg/Elbe
    Büchener Chaussee
    Tel: 452 (formerly 42)

Segelflugschule, Fischbeck, Hamburg-Fischbeck
    formerly Segelflugschule Fischbeck/Harburg
    Tel: Hamburg 378400
    Bahnstation: Hamburg-Neugraben

STANDARTE NO.	HQ LOCATION	COMPONENT UNITS (STÜRME)	
15	Hamburg 13 Oderfelderstr. 17 Tel: 521041/5 formerly Heimhuderstr. 5 Tel: 112335	1/15 2/15 3/15 4/15 5/15 6/15 7/15 8/15 9/15 10/15 11/15 * 12/15 * 13/15 * 14/15	Hamburg Hamburg Wandsbek Hamburg Bergedorf Altona Harburg Hamburg Hamburg Hamburg Hamburg-Bahrenfeld Hamburg-Grossborstel Hamburg/Finkenwärder Hamburg

16	Neumünster
	Strasse der SA 53
	Tel: Neumünster 2677
	  formerly
	Rathaus
	Tel: 540
		1/16
		2/16
		3/16
		4/16
		5/16
		6/16
		7/16
		
		8/16
		9/16
		10/16
		11/16
		12/16
		13/16
		14/16
			Kiel
			Schleswig
			Niebüll
			Neumünster
			Eutin
			Lübeck
			Ratzeburg
			  formerly: Lauenburg
			Bad Oldesloe
			Uetersen
			Itzehoe
			Heide
			Preetz
			Flensburg
			Kiel

* Entries marked thus were added, as amendments, in the German original.

CONFIDENTIAL

CONFIDENTIAL

GRUPPE 3 (Nordwest) (contd.)

STANDARTE NO.	HQ LOCATION	COMPONENT UNITS (STÜRME)	

17	Oldenburg i.O.
	Ministerialgebäude
	Tel: 6291
		1/17
		2/17
		3/17
		4/17
		5/17
		
		6/17
		7/17
		8/17
		
		9/17
		
		10/17
		11/17
		12/17
		
		13/17
			Oldenburg
			Bremen
			Bremen
			Bremen
			Bockhorn
			  formerly: Wilhelmshaven
			Norden
			Emden
			Quakenbrück
			  formerly: Vechta
			Quakenbrück
			  formerly: Bersenbrück
			Lingen
			Osnabrück
			Osnabrück
			  formerly: Haren-Ems
			Delmenhorst

18	Lüneburg
	Hindenburgstrasse 107a
	Tel: 4676
		1/18
		2/18
		3/18
		
		4/18
		5/18
		6/18
		7/18
		8/18
		
		9/18
		10/18
			Lüneburg
			Cuxhaven
			Wesermünde
			  formerly: Bremerhaven
			Rotenburg
			Walsrode
			Celle
			Lehrte
			Buchholz
			  formerly: Wenzendorf
			Gifhorn
			Buxtehude
			  formerly: Wilstedt

GRUPPE 4 (Berlin-Mark Brandenburg)

Headquarters: Berlin W 15
Metzstrasse 84
Tel: 249111

Reichsschule für Motorflugsport Rangsdorf, Kr. Teltow
    Flughafen
    Tel: 365/68

Technische Schule Fürstenberg/Oder
    Schönfliesser Chaussee
    Tel: 189

Segelflugschule Trebbin, Trebbin Kr. Teltow
    Tel: 479

Segelflugschule Rhinow, Rhinow
    Post Stoellen über Neustadt a.d. Dosse
    Tel: 162
    Bahnanschrift: Rhinow/Mark

STANDARTE NO.	HQ LOCATION	COMPONENT UNITS (STÜRME)	
22	Frankfurt/Oder Fürstenwalderstr. 56 Tel: 4362	1/22 2/22 3/22 4/22 5/22 6/22 7/22 8/22	Frankfurt/O Fürstenwalde Königsberg/Nm. Küstrin Landsberg/Warthe Soldin Zielenzig Drossen

23	Cottbus
	Berliner Str. 154
	Tel: 2727
		1/23
		2/23
		3/23
		4/23
		5/23
		6/23
		7/23
		8/23
		9/23
		10/23
		
		11/23
		12/23
		x
			Finsterwalde
			Senftenberg
			Lübbenau
			Cottbus
			Spremberg
			Forst/Stadt
			  formerly Forst/Land
			Sorau
			Guben
			Sommerfeld
			  formerly: Crossen x
			Züllichau x
			Meseritz x
			z.Zt. selbst. Truppe

CONFIDENTIAL

GRUPPE 4 (Berlin-Mark Brandenburg)
(contd.)

STANDARTE NO.	HQ LOCATION	COMPONENT UNITS (STÜRME)	
24	Neuruppin Steinstrasse 20 Tel: 2914	1/24 2/24 3/24	Perleberg Pritzwalk Neuruppin

		5/24
		6/24
		7/24
		8/24
		9/24
			Heinkel-Werk
			Angermünde
			  formerly: Oranienburg
			Eberswalde
			  formerly: Bad Freienwald
			  formerly: Neuenhagen
			           Erkner

25	Potsdam
	Türkstrasse 23
	Tel: 5137
		1/25
		
		2/25
		3/25
		4/25
		5/25
		6/25
		7/25
		8/25
		9/25
		10/25
		11/25
			Rathenow
			  formerly: Rhinow
			  formerly: Rangsdorf
			Falkensee
			Brandenburg
			Potsdam
			Beelitz
			Zossen
			Trebbin
			Beeskow
			Genshagen
			Jüterbog, Altes Lager

26	Berlin W 15 Motzstrasse 84 Tel: 249111	1/26 2/26 3/26 4/26 5/26 6/26 7/26 8/26	Bln-Reinickendorf Bln-Spandau Bln-Charlottenburg Berlin N 54 Bln-Wilmersdorf Bln-Schöneberg Bln-Steglitz formerly: Lichterfelde-West Berlin SW 68

27	Berlin SW 29
	Hasenheide 5/6
	Tel: 669730
		1/27
		2/27
		3/27
		4/27
		5/27
		6/27
		7/27
		8/27
		9/27
		11/27
			Bln-Pankow
			Berlin O 112
			Berlin SW 29
			Bln-Tempelhof
			Berlin SW 29
			Berlin O 112
			Bln-Friedrichshagen
			Erkner
			Berlin SW 29
			  formerly: Bln.-Tempelhof
			           Berlin SW 29

CONFIDENTIAL

CONFIDENTIAL

GRUPPE 5 (Wartheland)

Headquarters: Posen
Tiergartenstr. 6
Tel: 7417/18,
7545/46

Wehrsportschule Rossgarten, Posen
Tiergartenstrasse 6
Tel: 7417/18, 7545/46

STANDARTE NO.	HQ LOCATION	COMPONENT UNITS (STÜRME)	
119	Litzmannstadt Danziger-Str. 38 formerly Adolf-Hitler-Str. 106 Tel: 16539	1/119 Litzmannstadt 2/119 Litzmannstadt 3/119 Litzmannstadt 4/119 Pabianice 5/119 Ostrowo 6/119 Belgathof ✘ 8/119 Schildberg	
120	Hohensalza Friedrichstr. 30/I Tel: 443	1/120 Hohensalza 2/120 Gnesen ✘ 3/120 Altburgund ✘ 4/120 Bartolstein ✘ 5/120 Leslau ✘ 6/120 Kutno ✘ ✘ 8/120 Konin	

121	Posen
	Dr. Wilms-Str. 57
	Tel: 7121
		1/121 Posen
		2/121 Posen
		3/121 Posen
		4/121 Wreschen
		5/121 Grätz
		    formerly: Neutomischel
		6/121 Jarotschin
		    formerly: Pleschen
		7/121 Krotoschin
		8/121 Rawitsch
		9/121 Lissa
		10/121 Wolstein
		    formerly: Grätz
		11/121 Kolmar
		12/121 Schmiegel	

✘ Entries marked thus were added as amendments in the German original.

CONFIDENTIAL

CONFIDENTIAL

GRUPPE 6 (Schlesien)

Headquarters: Breslau
Hindenburgplatz 4
Tel: 82121, Nachtruf 80758

Flugzeugführerschule Breslau-Gandau
   Breslau 17, Flughafen
   Tel: 52011
   Bahnstation: Breslau-Mochbern

Reichsschule für Segelflugsport Grunau (Riesengebirge)
   Grunau über Hirschberg
   Tel: Hirschberg 3057

Segelflugschule Steinberg, Niederellguth,
   Post Gogolin-Land O.S.
   Tel: 244

STANDARTE NO.	HQ LOCATION	COMPONENT UNITS (STÜRME)	
29	Oppeln Sedanstr. 17 formerly Fleischerstr. 13 Tel: 4306	1/19	Gleiwitz formerly: Beuthen
		2/29	Loben formerly: Mechthal
		3/29	Gr. Strelitz formerly: Hindenburg
		4/29	Leobschütz formerly: Gleiwitz
		5/29	Kreutsburg formerly: Ratibor
		6/29	Neustadt formerly: Leobschütz
		7/29	Neisse formerly: Gr. Strelitz formerly: Krappitz
		8/29	Brieg formerly: Kreuzburg
		9/29	Oppeln
30	Breslau I Am Rathaus 25 Tel: 50371	1/30	Breslau
		2/30	Breslau
		3/30	Breslau
		4/30	Breslau
		5/30	Breslau ✶
		6/30	Breslau formerly: Neumark
		7/30	Wohlau formerly: Herrenstadt
		8/30	Ohlau formerly: Strahlen
		9/30	Oels formerly: Brieg
		10/30	Obernigk formerly: Oels
		11/30	Breslau-Lissa formerly: Trobnitz
		12/30	

✶ Ballor.

CONFIDENTIAL

CONFIDENTIAL

GRUPPE 6 (Schlesien) (contd.)

STANDARTE NO.	HQ LOCATION	COMPONENT UNITS (STÜRME)	

31	Waldenburg/Schles.
	Ring 1
	Tel: 1493
		1/31
		2/31
		3/31
		4/31
		5/31
		6/31
		7/31
		8/31
		
		9/31
		
		* 10/31
		* 11/31
			Trautenau
			Landeshut
			Waldenburg
			Braunau
			Glatz
			Hohenelbe
			Frankenstein
			Langenbielau
			  formerly: Reichenbach
			Freiburg
			  formerly: Schweidnitz
			Hirschberg
			Habelschwerdt

32	Görlitz Biegnitzer-Str. 33 Tel: 3895	1/32 2/32 3/32 4/32 5/32 6/32 7/32 8/32 9/32 10/32 11/32	Liegnitz Glogau Grünberg Sagan Weisswasser O/L Hoyerswerda Görlitz Lauban Bunzlau Haynau formerly: Hirschberg

33	Jägerndorf/M.-Schl.
	Adolf-Hitler-Platz 22
	Tel: 433
		1/33
		2/33
		3/33
		4/33
		5/33
		6/33
		7/33
		8/33
		9/33
		10/33
		11/33
		12/33
			Jägerndorf
			Troppau
			Neutitschein
			Bautsch
			Sternberg
			Freudenthal
			Freiwaldau
			M.-Schönberg
			Hohenstadt
			Zwittau
			Olmütz (Protektorat)
			  formerly: M. Ostrau
			    (Protektorat)

34	Kattowitz, O.-Schl.
	Grundmannstrasse 33
	Tel: 33449
		1/34
		2/34
		
		3/34
		4/34
		5/34
		6/34
		7/34
		8/34
		
		9/34
		
		10/34
		
		11/34
		
		12/34
		13/34
		14/34
			Tarnowitz
			Ruda
			  formerly: Morgenroth
			Schwientochlowitz
			Königshütte I
			Königshütte II
			Kattowitz
			Myslowitz
			Scharley
			  formerly: Nikolai
			Beuthen
			  formerly: Rybnik
			Mechtal
			  formerly: Teschen
			Hindenburg
			  formerly: Bielitz
			Radzionkau
			Kattowitz
			  formerly: Karwin

* Entries marked thus were added as amendments, in the German original.

CONFIDENTIAL

CONFIDENTIAL

GRUPPE 6 (Schlesien) (contd.)

STANDARTE NO.	HQ LOCATION	COMPONENT UNITS (STÜRME)	
35	Bielitz Beskidenstr. 3 Tel: 3025 formerly Dr. Goebbelsstr. 42 Tel: Bielitz 1424	1/35 2/35 3/35 4/35 5/35 6/35 7/35	Ratibor, O.S. Mährisch-Ostrau Rybnik Nikolai Karwin Teschen Bielitz

Note: All the information on this page was added, as an amendment, in the German original.

CONFIDENTIAL

GRUPPE 7 (Elbe-Saale)

Headquarters: Dresden A 16
Kreutzerstrasse 21
Tel: 64246

Flugzeugführerschule Dresden-Heller
　Dresden N 15
　Magazinstrasse 5
　Tel: Dresden 53032, 53544
　Güterbahnhof: Dresden N, Proviantnof

Reichsschule für Motorflug Chemnitz
　Chemnitz, Stollberger-Strasse 100
　Tel: 34233
　Güterbahnhof: Chemnitz-Kappel, Selbstabholer

Reichssegelflugschule Laucha/Unstrut
　Laucha-Dorndorf
　Tel: Laucha 187

Segelflugschule Grossrückerswalde Otto-Bräutigam-Schule
　bei Marienberg i. Sa.
　Tel: Marienberg i. Sa. 295

STANDARTE NO.	HQ LOCATION	COMPONENT UNITS (STURM)	
36	Halle/Saale Hermann-Göring-Strasse 1 Tel: 31676	1/36 2/36 3/36 4/36 5/36 6/36 7/36 8/36 9/36 10/36 11/36 12/36 13/36	Halle Halle Eilenburg Bitterfeld Eisleben Sangerhausen Naumburg Zeitz Merseburg Torgau Wittenberg Liebenwerda Halle

CONFIDENTIAL

CONFIDENTIAL

GRUPPE 7 (ELBE-SAALE)(contd)

STANDARTE NO.	HQ LOCATION	COMPONENT UNITS (STURME)	
37	Chemnitz Markt 12 Tel: 24129	1/37 2/37 3/37 4/37 5/37 6/37 7/37 8/37 9/37 10/37 11/37 12/37	Chemnitz Chemnitz Chemnitz Zschopau Oelsnitz i. E. Annaberg i. E. Aue i. Sa. Hartenstein Zwickau Meerane Falkenstein i. V. Plauen i. V.
38	Dresden A 16 Kreutzerstrasse 21 Tel: 64246	1/38 2/38 3/38 4/38 5/38 6/38 7/38 8/38 9/38 10/38 11/38 * 12/38	Freital Dresden Dresden Freiberg Bad Schandau Zittau Ebersbach Bautzen Langebrück Meissen Grossenhain Dresden
39	Leipzig C 1 Lessingstrasse 10, III Tel: 12300	1/39 2/39 3/39 4/39 5/39 6/39 7/39 8/39 * 9/39 * 10/39	Leipzig Leipzig Leipzig Leipzig Taucha Borna Döbeln Grimma Leipzig-Heiterblick (Sturm-Trupp) Burgstädt
40	Teplitz-Schönau Nordstrasse 5 Tel: 3651 (formerly: 498)	1/40 2/40 3/40 4/40 5/40 6/40 7/40 8/40 9/40 10/40 11/40 12/40 13/40 14/40 * 15/40 16/40 17/40 18/40	Gablonz Reichenberg Warnsdorf Leipa Tetschen Aussig Teplitz Dux Brüx Komotau Saaz Karlsbad Falkenau Graslitz Reichenberg Kaaden formerly: Lukau (selbär) Leitmeritz Prag (Protektorat)

* Entries marked thus were added as amendments, in the German original.

CONFIDENTIAL

CONFIDENTIAL

GRUPPE 8 (MITTE)

Headquarters: Eschwege
Niederhonerstr. 44
Tel: 2395/7

Reichsmodellflugschule Hoher Meissner, Velmeden, Bez. Kassel
  Tel: Grossalmerode 347
  Bahnstation: Velmeden b. Kassel

Reichssegelflugschule Wasserkuppe/Rhön, Gersfeld
  Tel: Gersfeld 207

Segelflugschule Harsberg, Lauterbach über Eisenach
  Tel: Mihla 25
  Bahnstation: Mihla-Werra

Segelflugschule Dörnberg, Zierenberg b. Kassel
  Tel: 175

STANDARTE NO.	HQ LOCATION	COMPONENT UNITS (STURME)	
43	Weimar Ludendorffstrasse 28 Tel: 889	1/43 Altenburg 2/43 Gera 3/43 Greiz 4/43 Schleiz 5/43 Saalfeld 6/43 Rudolstadt 7/43 Ilmenau 8/43 Arnstadt 9/43 Erfurt 10/43 Weimar 11/43 Jena 12/43 Sömmerda 13/43 Jena-Rödigen	
44	Gotha Friedrichstrasse 19 Tel: 2204	1/44 Sonneberg 2/44 Hildburghausen 3/44 Zella-Mehlis 4/44 Meiningen 5/44 Vacha 6/44 Schmalkalden 7/44 Waltershausen 8/44 Eisenach 9/44 Gotha 10/44 Langensalza 11/44 Heiligenstadt 12/44 Sondershausen 13/44 Nordhausen	

CONFIDENTIAL

CONFIDENTIAL

GRUPPE 8 (MITTE) (contd)

STANDARTE NO.	HQ LOCATION	COMPONENT UNITS (STURME)
45	Kassel Germaniastrasse 1 1½ Tel: 36097 (formerly Germaniastr. 31)	1/45 Eschwege 2/45 Bebra 3/45 Fulda 4/45 Homberg 5/45 Harburg 6/45 Bad Wildungen 7/45 Hofgeismar 8/45 Kassel 9/45 Kassel

CONFIDENTIAL

GRUPPE 9 (Weser-Elbe)

Headquarters: Hannover
Walderseestr. 1
Tel: 60541/42

Technische Schule Hannover, Stader Chausse 34
Tel: 63398

Reichssegelflugschule Ith, Post Alfeld Leine-Land
    Tel: Eschershausen über Holzminden 131
    Bahnstation für Personen: Schürfoldendorf
      formerly: Bahnstation f. Personen: Stadt Oldendorf
    Güterbhf.: Eschershausen

Segelflugschule Salzgitter (formerly: G tter am Berge)
    Kreis Salzgitter/Harz
    Tel: 565 Salzgitter

Segelflugschule Balenstedt/Harz
    Tel: 475
    Bahnstation: Ballenstedt-W.

STANDARTE NO.	HQ LOCATION	COMPONENT UNITS (STÜRME)	
50	Hannover Walderseestrasse 1 Tel: 60541/42	1/50 2/50 3/50 4/50 5/50 6/50 7/50 8/50 9/50 10/50 11/50 12/50 13/50 14/50 15/50 16/50 17/50 * 18/50	Hannover Hannover Hannover Peine Braunschweig Braunschweig Wolfenbüttel Helmstedt Schöningen Goslar Seesen Göttingen Northeim Gronau formerly: Alfeld/Leine Holzminden Nienburg Hildesheim Salzgitter
52	Magdeburg Grosse Klosterstr. 16 Tel: 30888	1/52 2/52 3/52 4/52 5/52 6/52 7/52 8/52 9/52 10/52	Magdeburg Magdeburg Burg Haldensleben Gardelegen Salzwedel Stendal Oschersleben formerly: Stendal Westeregeln Genthin

* Entry marked thus was added as an amendment in the German original.

CONFIDENTIAL

CONFIDENTIAL

GRUPPE 9 (Weser-Elbe) (contd.)

STANDARTE NO.	HQ LOCATION	COMPONENT UNITS (STÜRME)	

53	Dessau
	Kaiserstr. 4
	  formerly
	Steneschestr. 148/50
	Tel: 5262
		1/53
		2/53
		3/53
		4/53
		5/53
		6/53
		7/53
		8/53
		9/53
		10/53
		11/53
			Dessau
			  formerly: Koswig
			Zerbst
			Köthen
			Schönebeck
			Bernburg
			Stassfurt
			Aschersleben
			Thale
			Halberstadt
			Wernigerode

CONFIDENTIAL

GRUPPE 10 (Westfalen)

Headquarters: Dortmund 1
1 Kampstrasse 88-94
Tel: 35741

Flugzeugführerschule (M) Gelsenkirchen,
    Buer, Flughafen
    Tel: Gelsenkirchen 30755
    Bahnstation: Buer-Nord

Flugzeugführerschule Bielefeld
    Tel: Bielefeld 1944
    Post: Windelsbleiche, Flughafen
    Güterbahnhof: Bielefeld-Windelsbleiche

Segelflugschule Schüren über Meschede i. Westf.
    Tel: Reiste 44
    Bahnstation: Wenemen

Segelflugschule Borkenberge,
    Bahnstation: Dülmen in Westfalen
    Tel: 424

Technische Schule Rehme, Rehme b. Bad Oeynhausen,
    Vlothoer Strasse 44
    Tel: Bad Oeynhausen 2543
    Bahnstation: Bad Oeynhausen

STANDARTE NO.	HQ LOCATION	COMPONENT UNITS (STÜRME)	
57	Dortmund Stubengasse 29 Tel: 37028	1/57	Dortmund
		2/57	Dortmund
		3/57	Iserlohn formerly: Bochum
		4/57	Lippstadt formerly: W.Eickel
		5/57	Hattingen
		6/57	Hagen
		7/57	Schwerte
		8/57	Gevelsberg
		* 9/57	Neheim
		*10/57	Hamm
58	Arnsberg Bahnhofstrasse Arbeitsamt Arnsberg Tel: 580	1/58	Arnsberg formerly: Iserlohn
		2/58	Werdohl
		3/58	Lüdenscheid
		4/58	Erndtebrück formerly: Lippstadt
		5/58	Attendorn
		6/58	Meschede
		7/58	Siegen formerly: Ferndorf
		8/58	Brilon formerly: Hamm
		9/58	formerly: Neheim

* Entries marked thus were added as amendments, in the German original.

CONFIDENTIAL

CONFIDENTIAL

GRUPPE 10 (Westfalen) (contd.)

STANDARTE NO.	HQ LOCATION	COMPONENT UNITS (STÜRME)	

59	Münster/Westf.
	Kronprinzenstr. 8
	Tel: 23503
		1/59
		2/59
		3/59
		4/59
		5/59
		6/59
		
		7/59
		
		8/59
		9/59
		10/59
		
		* 11/59
		* 12/59
			Ahlen
			Münster
			Greven
			Rheine
			Epe
			Bocholt
			  formerly: Recklinghausen
			Coesfeld
			  formerly: Gladbeck
			  formerly: Gelsenkirchen
			  formerly: Gelsenkirchen
			Warendorf
			  formerly: Wattenscheid
			Ibbenbüren
			Burgsteinfurt

60	Bielefeld/Westf.
	Herforderstr. 8
	Tel: 4608
	  formerly
	Detmold
	Doktorweg 6
	Tel: 2345
		1/60
		2/60
		3/60
		4/60
		
		5/60
		6/60
		7/60
		8/60
		9/60
		10/60
		11/60
		*12/60
			Detmold
			Paderborn
			Warburg
			Bückeburg
			  formerly: Nienstädt
			Minden
			Herford
			Bielefeld
			Gütersloh
			Lübbecke
			Lemgo
			Bünde
			Brackwede

*61	* Recklinghausen Strasse der SA 22 Tel: 3223	* 1/61 * 2/61 * 3/61 * 4/61 * 5/61 * 6/61 * 7/61 * 8/61 * 9/61 *10/61 *11/61 *12/61	Castrop Herne Bochum Wanne-Eickel Recklinghausen Gladbeck Gelsenkirchen Gelsenkirchen Wattenscheid Gelsenkirchen-Buer

* Entries marked thus were added as amendments, in the German original.

CONFIDENTIAL

GRUPPE 11 (Hessen-Moselland)
formerly: (Hessen-Westm.)

Headquarters: Frankfurt/Main
Fellnerstr. 5
Tel: 50206

Flugzeugführerschule (M), Frankfurt-Rebstock, Flughafen
  Tel: 77704
  Bahnstation: Frankfurt a. M., Hauptgtbhf.

Segelflugschule Hummerich, Kruft b. Andernach
  Tel: Andernach 314
  Bahnstation: Kruft b. Andernach
    formerly: Plaidt b. Andernach

STANDARTE NO.	HQ LOCATION	COMPONENT UNITS (STÜRME)	
72	Koblenz Gerichtsstr. 3 Tel: 4226 formerly Schloss-Str. 9 Tel: 7320	1/72 2/72 3/72 4/72 5/72 6/72 7/72	Koblenz Bad Kreuznach formerly: Trier formerly: Tr. Trarbach Wittlich Neuwied formerly: Andernach Wissen/Sieg formerly: Kinz/Rh. formerly: Trier Bitburg (z.Zt. selbst. Trupp)
75	Frankfurt/Main Fellnerstr. 6 Tel: 50206 formerly Mainzer Landstr. 14 Tel: 74833	1/75 2/75 3/75 4/75 5/75 6/75 7/75 8/75 9/75 10/75 11/75 12/75	Frankfurt a.M. Frankfurt a.M. Bad Homburg Butzbach Gelnhausen Giessen Wetzlar Diez/Lahn Montabaur Hirzenhain Wiesbaden Hanau
77	Darmstadt Rheinstr. 75 Tel: 4321 formerly Gutenbergstr. 36 Tel: 4321	1/77 2/77 3/77 4/77 5/77 6/77 7/77 8/77	Darmstadt Offenbach/M Dieburg Heppenheim Rüsselsheim Worms Mainz Erbach

(Note: All remaining information on this page was added, as an amendment, in the German original)

78	Luxenburg Prinzenring 43 Tel: 3828 Postsendungen an: Deutscher Luftsportverband, Luxenburg	1/78 2/78 3/78 4/78 5/78 6/78	Luxenburg Wilz Esch/Alzig Trier, s. Trupp Bitburg, s. Trupp Wittlich

CONFIDENTIAL

CONFIDENTIAL

GRUPPE 12 (Niederrhein)

Headquarters: Essen
Alfredstr. 61/63
Tel: 44421

Flugzeugführerschule (M),
  München-Gladbach, Flughafen Holterheide
  Tel: 23551
  Güterbahnhof: München-Gladbach-Speick

Motorflugzeugführerschule Vogelsang (formerly Motorflugzeugschule Vogelsang)
  Ordensburg bei Gemünd, Eifel
  Tel: Gemünd 281
  Bahnstation: Gemünd/Eifel

Flugzeugführerschule Köln,
  Köln-Butzweilerhof, Flughafen
  Tel: Köln 58201
  Güterbahnhof: Köln-Gereon

STANDARTE NO.	HQ LOCATION	COMPONENT UNITS (STÜRME)	
65	Köln Hohenstaufenring 45 Tel: 216003 formerly Stadtwaldgürtel 12 Tel: 45205	1/65 2/65 3/65 4/65 5/65 6/65 7/65 8/65 9/65 10/65	Köln Köln Bonn Siegburg Wipperfürth Euskirchen formerly: Münstereifel Aachen Jülich Düren Eupen (Note: this entry was added as an amendment in the German original)
66	Düsseldorf Kapellstrasse 10 Tel: 37656	1/66 2/66 4/66 5/66 6/66 7/66 8/66 9/66 10/66 11/66 12/66 13/66	Düsseldorf Düsseldorf Krefeld Krefeld M.-Gladbach Kempen Neuss Langenberg Wuppertal Wuppertal Solingen Remscheid Leverkusen
67	Duisburg Flughafen Tel: 20939	1/67 2/67 3/67 4/67 5/67 6/67 7/67 8/67	Essen Mülheim Duisburg Oberhausen Dinslaken Moers Emmerich Kleve

CONFIDENTIAL

CONFIDENTIAL

GRUPPE 13 (Main-Donau)

Headquarters: Nürnberg O
Theodorstrasse 1
Tel: 53051

Technische Schule Dinkelsbühl,
    Fichtelbergweg 3
    Tel: 300

Reichsmodellflugschule (formerly Flugmodellbauschule) Rothenburg o.d.T.
    Tel: 31

Segelflugschule Hesselberg,
    Gerolfingen, Wassertrüdingen/Mittelfranken
    Tel: Wittelshofen 21
    Bahnstation: Wassertrüdingen

STANDARTE NO.	HQ LOCATION	COMPONENT UNITS (STÜRME)	
87	Nürnberg O Gleisbühlstr. 12 formerly Königstrasse 2 Tel: 27305	1/87 2/87 3/87 4/87 5/87 6/87 7/87 8/87 9/87 10/87	Nürnberg Nürnberg Fürth Erlangen Lauf Schwabach Weissenburg i.B. Ansbach Neustadt/Aisch Fürth i.B.
88	Würzburg Schönleinstr. 9 formerly Tröltschstrasse 4 Tel: 5740	1/88 2/88 3/88 4/88 5/88 6/88 7/88 8/88 9/88	Würzburg Kitzingen Aschaffenburg Bad Kissingen Schweinfurt Würzburg Würzburg Miltenberg Ostheim
89	Kulmbach Lichtenfelser Str. 1 Tel: 6040	1/89 2/89 3/89 4/89 5/89 6/89 7/89 8/89 9/89 10/89 11/89 12/89	Bayreuth Kulmbach Herzogenaurach Bamberg Coburg Münchberg Hof/Bay. Selb Marktredwitz Waldsassen Weiden Vilseck

CONFIDENTIAL

CONFIDENTIAL

GRUPPE 13 (Main-Donau) (contd.)

STANDARTE NO.	HQ LOCATION	COMPONENT UNITS (STÜRME)	
90	Regensburg Landshuter Str. 18 Tel: 3814	1/90 2/90 3/90 4/90 5/90 6/90 7/90 8/90 9/90 10/90	Regensburg Straubing Schwandorf Passau Landshut Pfarrkirchen Deggendorf Regensburg Wallern Regensburg/Obertraubling
91	Eger Holldorfstrasse 9 Tel: 905	1/91 2/91 3/91 4/91 5/91 6/91 7/91 8/91 9/91	Eger Asch Rossbach Fleissen Franzensbad Marienbad Pilsen formerly: Mies Tachau Plan

CONFIDENTIAL

CONFIDENTIAL

GRUPPE 14 (Hochland)

Headquarters: München 2 NW
Theresienstrasse 84
Tel: 51704

Motorflugzeugführerschule (formerly Motorflugschule) Sonthofen
  Kempten-Durach bei der Ordensburg Sonthofen
  Bahnstation: Durach bei Kempten, Allg. Flughafen
  Tel: Sonthofen 3402

Segelflugschule Schwangau i. Allg.
  Tel: Füssen 305
  Bahnstation: Füssen/Allg.

STANDARTE NO.	HQ LOCATION	COMPONENT UNITS (STÜRME)	
94	München Leopoldstrasse 50 Tel: 35204	1/94 2/94 3/94 4/94 5/94 6/94 7/94 8/94 9/94 10/94 11/94 12/94 14/94	München München München Pasing München Schleissheim München München Starnberg Landsberg Freising Schrobenhausen Ingolstadt

95/96	Augsburg
	Klinkerberg 7
	Tel: 7436
		1/95
		2/95
		3/95
		4/95
		5/95
		6/95
		7/95
		8/95
		9/95
		10/95
		
		1/96
		2/96
		3/96
		4/96
		5/96
		6/96
		
		7/96
			Augsburg
			Augsburg
			Augsburg
			Augsburg
			Günzburg
			Lauingen
			Nördlingen
			Neuburg a.D.
			  formerly: Leipheim
			Gablingen
			
			Neu-Ulm
			Memmingen
			Mindelheim
			Kaufbeuren
			Kempten
			Blaichach
			  formerly: Oberstdorf
			Füssen

CONFIDENTIAL

CONFIDENTIAL

GRUPPE 14 (Hochland) (contd.)

STANDARTE NO.	HQ LOCATION	COMPONENT UNITS (STÜRME)	
97	Prien am Chiemsee Von-Epp-Strasse 3 Tel: 272	1/97 2/97 3/97 4/97 5/97	Wolfrahtsh. Holzkirchen Rosenheim Prien Traunstein
		7/97 8/97 9/97 10/97	Wasserburg Mühldorf Garm.-Partenk. Weilheim
98	Innsbruck Müllerstrasse 13/2 Tel: 2112	1/98 2/98	Innsbruck Kufstein
		4/98 5/98	Lustenau Bregenz

CONFIDENTIAL

CONFIDENTIAL

GRUPPE 15 (Württemberg) (formerly Schwaben)

Headquarters: Stuttgart O
Neckarstrasse 195
Tel: 42141/42

Technische Schule Esslingen am Neckar
    Zollbergstrasse 1
    Tel: 7938

Reichsschule für Segelflugsport - Hornberg, Schwäb. Gmünd
    Tel: Schw.-Gmünd 2777
    Bahnstation: Weissenstein
               Schwäb.-Gmünd

Segelflugschule Teck/Dettingen
    Tel: Kirchheim 505
    Bahnstation: Teck/Dettingen

STANDARTE NO.	HQ LOCATION	COMPONENT UNITS (STÜRME)	
101	Stuttgart W Rosenbergstrasse 1 Tel: 23339	1/101 2/101 3/101 4/101 5/101 6/101 7/101 8/101	Stuttgart Stuttgart Stuttgart Wildbad Stuttgart (Ballon) Böblingen-Sindelfingen Tübingen Esslingen
102	Schwäb. Hall Markplatz Tel: 377	1/102 2/102 3/102 4/102 5/102 6/102 7/102 8/102 9/102 10/102	Heilbronn Schw.-Hall Bad Mergenth. Vaihingen Bietigheim Schw.-Gmünd Aalen Göppingen Waiblingen Heidenheim

103	Ulm
	Tel: 5183
	  formerly
	Kirchheim/Teck
	Altes Schloss
	Tel: 464
		1/103
		2/103
		3/103
		
		4/103
		5/103
		6/103
		7/103
		8/103
		9/103
		
		10/103
		11/103
			Friedrichshafen
			Wangen i. Allg.
			Friedrichshafen-
			  Ravensburg
			Saulgau
			Biberach
			Ulm
			Kirchheim-Tack
			Reutlingen
			Freudenstadt/Schwarzwald
			  formerly: Dornstetten
			Balingen
			Schwenningen

CONFIDENTIAL

CONFIDENTIAL

GRUPPE 16 (Südwest)

Headquarters: Strassburg/Elsass
Schwarzwaldstr.
Tel: 27702-4
formerly Karlsruhe
Leopoldplatz 7.a
Tel: 8355/56
* Fracht- u. Eilgutsendungen: Bahnhof
Strassburg-Kronenburg

Flugzeugführerschule Freiburg/Br., (M),
   Adolf-Hitler-Str. 70
   Tel: 8227

Flugzeugführerschule Karlsruhe/Baden, Flughafen
   Tel: 8336
   Güterbahnhof: Karlsruhe-West

STANDARTE NO.	HQ LOCATION	COMPONENT UNITS (STÜRME)	
80	Mannheim-Neuostheim formerly Flughafen, Haus der Flieger 05, 15, Tel: 28002	1/80 2/80 3/80 4/80 5/80 6/80 7/80 8/80 * 9/80 * 10/80	T'bischofsheim Mosbach Heidelberg Mannheim-Süd Bruchsal Karlsruhe Durlach Pforzheim Mannheim-Nord Schwetzingen
81	Saarbrücken formerly Neustadt a.d.W. Landauer Strasse 53 Tel: 3031	1/81 2/81 3/81 4/81 5/81 6/81 7/81 8/81 9/81 10/81 11/81 12/81	Gernersheim L'hafen Kaiserslautern Pirmasens Homburg/Saar St. Ingbert Ottweiler Landsweiler Freidrichsthal Saarbrücken Völklingen Saarlautern

82	Villingen/Schw.
	Wehrstr. 1
	formerly
	Mülhausen im Elsass
	formerly
	Villingen/Schw.
	Klosterring 1
		1/82
		
		2/82
		
		3/82
		
		4/82
		5/82
		6/82
		7/82
		8/82
		9/82
		* 10/82
		* 11/82
		* 12/82
		* 13/82
			Rappoltsweiler
			  formerly: Rastatt
			Kolmar
			  formerly: Offenburg
			Gebweiler
			  formerly: Haslach i. K.
			Freiburg/Br.
			Lörrach
			z.Zt. Erzingen
			Donaueschingen
			Singen a. H.
			Konstanz
			Thann
			Altkirch
			Mülhausen
			Villingen

* Entries marked thus were added as amendments, in the German original

CONFIDENTIAL
E28

CONFIDENTIAL

GRUPPE 16 (Südwest) (contd.)

STANDARTE NO.	HQ LOCATION	COMPONENT UNITS (STÜRME)	
83	Strassburg Pioniergasse 2a Tel: 20301	1/83 2/83 3/83 4/83 5/83 6/83 7/83 8/83 9/83 10/83 11/83 12/83	Rastatt Offenburg Haslach Weissenburg Zabern Hagenau Strassburg Molsheim Erstein Schlettstadt Bühl
84	Metz (Deutscher-Luftsport- verband, Lothringen) Rosenstr. 18 Tel: 2428	1/84 2/84 3/84 4/84 5/84 6/84 7/84 8/84 9/84	Metz Metz Hayingen Diedenhofen Kreuzwald Merlenbach Saargemünd Saarburg Wich

Note: All information on this page was added as an amendment in the German original.

CONFIDENTIAL

GRUPPE 17 (Donau-Alpenland) (formerly Ostmark)

Headquarters: Wien III
Metternichgasse 6
Tel: U 19575

Flugzeugführerschule (M) Aigen im Emsthal, Ostmark
   Bahnstation: Wörschach-Schwefelbad (Ostamrk)
   Tel: Aigen 4 Fliegerhorstkommandantur

Reichssegelflugschule Spitzerberg
   Prellenkirchen/Dt. Altenburg a.d.D.
   Tel: Prellenkirchen Niederdonau 7
   Bahnstation: Deutsch-Altenburg/Niederdonau

Hochalpine Segelflugschule Zell a. See

STANDARTE NO.	HQ LOCATION	COMPONENT UNITS (STÜRME)	
111	Linz a.d.D.	1/111	Linz
	Kroatengasse 21	2/111	Linz
	Tel: 24400	3/111	Eferding
	formerly: 7100	4/111	Kirchdorf
		5/111	Gmunden
		6/111	Steyregg
		7/111	Steyr
		8/111	Freistadt
		9/111	Lenzing
		10/111	Braunau
		11/111	Schärding
		12/111	Krumau
		13/111	Wels
		14/111	Budweis (Protektorat)
		15/111	Gratzen
		16/111)	formerly:
		17/111)	Sturmbann Salzburg
112	Wien IX	1/112	Wien
	Währinger Strasse 17	2/112	Wien
	Tel: A 23261	3/112	Wien
		4/112	Wien
		5/112	Wien
		6/112	Wien
		7/112	Wien
		8/112	Wien
		10/112	Wien
		12/112	Wien
		13/112	Wien
113	Klagenfurt	1/113	Klagenfurt
	Sterneckstrasse 11	2/113	Völkermarkt (s. Tr.)
	Tel: 313	3/113	St. Veit a. Glan
		4/113	Lienz
		6/113	Villach
		7/113	Wolfsberg

CONFIDENTIAL

CONFIDENTIAL

GRUPPE 17 (Donau-Alpenland) (contd.)

STANDARTE NO.	HQ LOCATION	COMPONENT UNITS (STÜRME)
114	Znaim Salisplatz 17 Tel: 266	1/114 Znaim 2/114 Miplitz formerly: Grussbach 3/114 Nikolsburg 4/114 Neubistritz 5/114 Gmünd 6/114 Horn 7/114 Brünn-Nord (Protektorat) 8/114 Brünn-Süd (Protektorat) 9/114 Iglau (Protektorat) * 10/114 Zlabings * 11/114 Zlin (s. Tr.)
115	Graz Krefelder Strasse 31 Tel: 5284	1/115 Graz 2/115 Graz 3/115 Leibnitz 4/115 Leoben 5/115 Stainach 6/115 Mürzzuschlag 7/115 Pinkafeld

116	Wien I
	Joh.-Seb.-Gasse 17
	Tel: 28234
		1/16 Krems
		2 116 Melk
		3/116 Amstetten
		4/116 Wilhelmsburg
		5/116 Wr.-Neustadt
		6/116 Baden
		7/116 Hainburg
		8/116 Engerau
		9/116 Stockerau
		10/116 Strahshof
		    formerly: Dtsch. Wagram
		* 11/116 St. Pölten
		
		17/116 Piesting
		    formerly: Wr.-Neustadt

* Sturmbann 201	Salzburg	* 1/201 Salzburg * 2/201 Salzburg

* Entries marked thus were added as amendments in the German original.

CONFIDENTIAL

CONFIDENTIAL

BRIGADE 125 (Weichselland)

Headquarters: Danzig
Schichaugasse 6
formerly
Karrenwall 7
Tel: 22241

Flugzeugführerschule Danzig-Langfuhr
Kleiner Hammerweg 54
Tel: Danzig 427

STANDARTE NO.	HQ LOCATION	COMPONENT UNITS (STÜRME)	
125 "Fritz Schwarz"	Danzig Karrenwall 7 Tel: 22241	1/125	Danzig
		2/125	Danzig-Langfuhr
		3/125	Danzig-Langfuhr
		4/125	Zoppot
		5/125	Tiegenhof
		6/125	Elbing
		7/125	Marienburg
		8/125	Riesenburg
		9/125	Dirschau
		10/125	Gotenhafen
		13/125	Karthaus
		14/125	Pr. Stargard
126	Bromberg Adolf-Hitler-Strasse 92 Tel: 3608	1/126	Bromberg
		2/126	Thorn
		3/126	Zempelburg
		4/126	Thorn
		5/126	Graudenz
		6/126	Wirsitz
		7/126	Kulm
		8/126	Strasburg
		* 9/126	Konitz
		* 10/126	Leipe

* Entries marked thus were added as amendments in the German original

---

Einheit GG (General Gouvernement)

Sturm 1/GG Krakau
2/GG Mielec
3/GG Tschenstochau
4/GG Radom
5/GG Warschau
6/GG Lemberg

Note: the whole of the entry "Einheit GG" (which is independent, not subordinate to any Gruppe) was added, as an amendment, in the German original.

An unrivalled insight into the Nazi State

Extremely rare historic wartime studies of Nazi Germany's Paramilitary Wings, Organisations, Documents and War Criminals, that were compiled by Supreme Headquarters Allied Expeditionary Forces (SHAEF) and other more clandestine agencies.

These reports illustrate what the Allies had learned about the Nazi state prior to the eventual disarming and demobilisation of German military forces, and also in assisting in the hunting of wanted war criminals and interrogation of those accused of collaborating with the German occupation authorities.

Full colour as in the original works as appropriate, unedited, containing some or all of the following: uniforms and insignia (colour uniform plates), a listing of personalities holding, details of organisation, ranks, orders of battle and wartime activities, and identity and other documents carried by German citizens and alien labour within the Third Reich, and of the citizens of Nazi-occupied Holland, Belgium and Luxembourg (colour plates).

IDENTITY DOCUMENTS IN GERMANY 1944

SB: 9781474536745

HB: 9781474536752

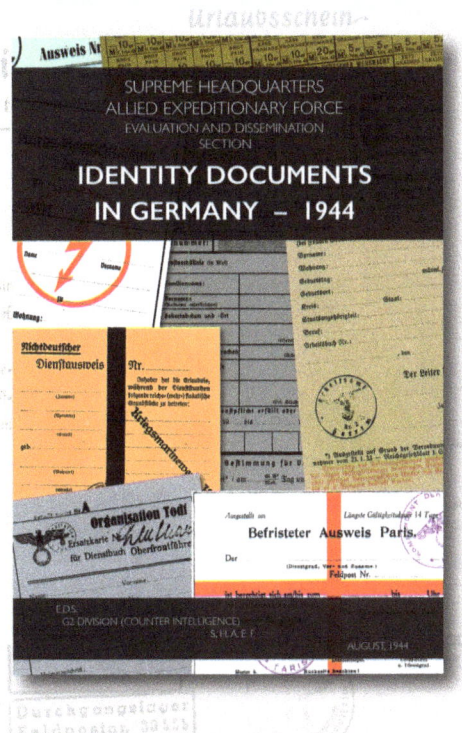

IDENTITY DOCUMENTS IN HOLLAND, BELGIUM AND LUXEMBOURG

SB: 9781474536882

HB: 9781474536899

THE NSKK OF THE NSDAP

Nationalsozialistisches Kraftfahrkorps – National Socialist Motor Corps

SB: 9781474536806

HB: 9781474536813

THE NSFK OF THE NSDAP

Nationalsozialistisches Fliegerkorps – National Socialist Flyers Corps

SB: 9781474536820

HB: 9781474536837

THE SA OF THE NAZI PARTY

Die Sturmabteilung Der NSDAP – Brownshirt or Storm Troop Formations

SB: 9781474536769

HB: 9781474536776

THE HITLER JUGEND
The Hitler Youth Organisation

SB: 9781474536844

HB: 9781474536851

HANDBOOK OF THE ORGANISATION TODT
The Civil And Military Engineering Organisation of Nazi Germany

SB: 9781474536783

HB: 9781474536790

THE REICHSARBEITSDIENST
Reichsarbeitsdienst (RAD) The German Labour Service

SB: 9781474536868

HB: 9781474536875

THE GERMAN POLICE

SB: 9781843425946

HB: 9781474536905

CROWCASS
Central Registry of War Criminals and Security Suspects. Wanted Lists
(The Nazi Hunter's Bible)

SB: 9781845742768

HB: 9781845742775

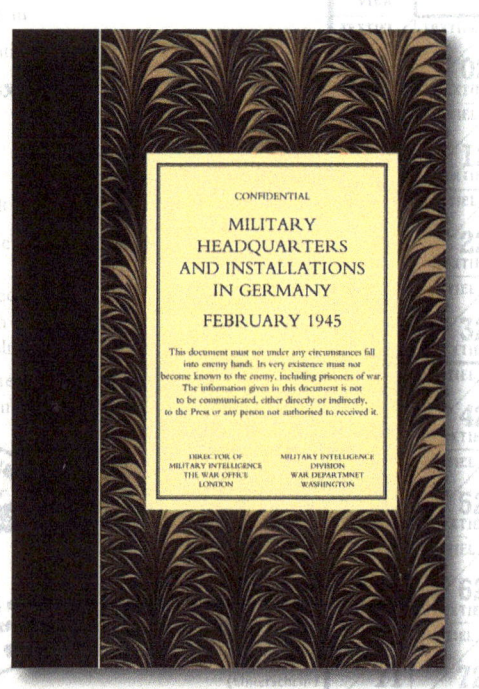

MILITARY HEADQUARTERS AND INSTALLATIONS IN GERMANY

SB: 9781843424420

www.ingramcontent.com/pod-product-compliance
Lightning Source LLC
Chambersburg PA
CBHW061538010526
44111CB00025B/2963